PAMELA SCOTT

Far ABOVE RUBIES

THE POWER OF CHRIST'S VIRTUE IN YOU

FAR ABOVE RUBIES
The Power of Christ's Virtue In You

214-326-5033
DrPamela3126@gmail.com
www.eaglesiti.org / www.tenworldwide.org

ISBN 978-1-949826-67-8

Published by: EAGLES GLOBAL BOOKS | Plano, Texas

Cover and interior designed by PublishAffordably.com | (773) 783-2981

℘

ENDORSEMENTS

Far Above Rubies is treasure chest filled with jewels that capture the true meaning of what it means to be a Chayil woman. This book aids in the growth, and transformation for all women so they can grow beyond even their current perception of femininity. Through this transformative study, God's Chayil women will even experience healing in areas that only women would understand. Upon reading this book the reader is sure to be restored, uplifted, and empowered to advance into a new Chayil life.

Katrina R. Carter
TEN Team Director, Eagles International Training Institute
Leader, International Company of Chayil Women, Ohio

℘

This book, *Far Above Rubies*, is a must read for every woman who wants to understand and walk into their full potential. Dr. Scott's insight and prophetic revelation takes the reader into a powerful in-depth understanding of our true worth as Chayil woman. I thank God for the Chayil force operating in Dr. Scott and the impact she has had throughout the world equipping, activating and releasing the Chayil Force within.

Graced with a supernatural global perspective, she reminds us all that our worth is *"Far Above Rubies."* Get ready for the Chayil force to arise within you!

Janine Dailey
International Director, Eagles International Training Institute
Vice President, Pine Manor College

૪૭

"Far Above Rubies" is more than just a book, it is an excellent manual for unearthing how precious and resilient you are in the sight of God. There is no doubt that as you read it's pages, you will discover the invaluable truths, wisdom and revelation that Dr. Pamela Scott has shared. I highly recommend this book. It will empower you to walk in Chayil Strength and Power.

Janelle Jagdeo
Co-founder of Adonai Arts Academy
Tortola, British Virgin Islands

૪૭

The Almighty God, the Great I am, the only King of the universe, is raising an army of virtuous women, powerful queens, worship warriors who are humble, sensitive to the heart of God and sensitive to the needs of others, but firm in their convictions of the kingdom. Women with the irrefutable identity as daughters of royalty and bearers of the divine wisdom, are also called to multiply riches. We are capable of transforming the world with the resurrection power received from the throne as our inheritance of the Redeemer, Jesus Christ. We are women of fire who destroy all the forces of the enemy that try to threaten our position in heavenly places. Through "*Far Above Rubies*", the Holy Spirit, using the heart and wisdom of a virtuous woman, Pamela Scott, will elevate you to another dimension of His CHAYIL glory. Prepare! This is your time of resurgence! From Zion, from the heights, God will hand you the scepter, the rod of His authority, so you can govern. He will dress you with His mantle of power to dominate and to defeat every enemy while you dwell confident and victorious in the chambers of the KING. The Lord will extend His mighty scepter from Zion, saying, "Rule in the midst of your enemies!"

Lilly Rodríguez
Flames of Freedom Ministry
Puerto Rico

&

Far Above Rubies Is an excellent book. I encourage ALL women to read this book. It will help you tap into and realize who you really are. If you are ready, I mean truly ready to be catapulted into your "Chayil" self, then I admonish you to read this book! May the Chayil force be with you..and shine through you!

ShaVonne Thomas
Administrative Director
Eagles International Training Institute

Far Above Rubies

ॐ

TABLE OF CONTENTS

Introduction... vii

Chapter 1
Identity 1

Chapter 2
The VIRTUE of Christ 4

Chapter 3
The Virtue of FORCE 11

Chapter 4
The Virtue of Christ's ARMY 15

Chapter 5
The Virtue of WEALTH..................................... 19

Chapter 6
The Virtue of WEALTH Part 2 23

Chapter 7
The Virtue of WEALTH Part 3 31

Chapter 8
Your Chayil WEALTH DECREE 40

Chapter 9
Christ's Virtue of VALOR.................................. 50

Chapter 10
10 Christ's Virtue of STRENGTH 56

Chapter 11
The Virtue of Christ's POWER 62

Chapter 12
VALIANT - A Virtue of Christ 68

Chapter 13
The Virtue of WAR 76

Chapter 14
The Virtue of WORSHIP 81

Chapter 15
WISDOM - The Virtue of Christ 84

Chapter 16
The LAW OF KINDNESS is the Virtue of Christ 92

Chapter 17
The Virtue of the Fear of the Lord 100

Chapter 18
The Many Virtues of Christ 104

Chapter 19
The Virtue of CHAYIL ACCELERATION 109

Chapter 20
The Virtue of the Chayil MANDATE 117

Conclusion 123

International Company of Chayil Women 127

ABOUT ICCW 129

INTRODUCTION

The virtuous woman of Proverbs 31 is a wonderful picture to help us learn who we are in Christ. The word virtuous is the word Chayil. Living as a Chayil woman can become our daily lifestyle.

We are a force because of the Christ who lives in us. We are a powerful, mighty, fearless army of worshippers because of the Christ who lives in us. It is His life and His virtue that gives us life and Chayil virtue.

2 Peter 1:2-8
"Grace and peace be multiplied unto you through the knowledge of God, and of Jesus our Lord,

According as His divine power hath given unto us all things that pertain unto life and godliness, through the knowledge of Him that hath called us to glory and virtue:

Whereby are given unto us exceeding great and precious promises: that by these ye might be partakers of the divine nature, having escaped the corruption that is in the world through lust."

And beside this, giving all diligence, add to your faith

virtue; and to virtue knowledge;

And to knowledge temperance; and to temperance patience; and to patience godliness;

And to godliness brotherly kindness; and to brotherly kindness charity.

For if these things be in you, and abound, they make you that ye shall neither be barren nor unfruitful in the knowledge of our Lord Jesus Christ."

We have been called to virtue. We are to add virtue to our faith. As a virtuous women, may the victorious, Chayil anointing of God be your daily reality as you live in the power of Christ's virtues in you!

ಐ

~ Chapter One ~

IDENTITY

Ladies, the time has come for us to arise and be the beautiful, graceful, strong warriors God has created us to be! There is a warfare over our identity. We need to know who we are and whose we are and step into the truth of that identity.

Many things come to try to move us away from the truth of who we are in Christ. As His dearly beloved, born of God, we are the apple of His eye and He loves us dearly!

> *Proverbs 31:10 says,*
> *"Who can find a virtuous woman? for her price is far above rubies."*

The word virtuous is the Hebrew word Chayil! God wants us to know that we are Chayil women with a value far above even the most precious earthly gem. When we embrace everything Chayil represents and submit to the Chayil identity God has for us, then God can unlock His destiny within us.

Past mistakes, situations or circumstances can often cause us to have a skewed perception of who we really are. These same identifiers can even cause others not to see the true value that is in us.

The truth of the Chayil identify will cause us to be determined that we will no longer submit to the identity others try to put on us.

The word Chayil means force, army, wealth, virtue, valor, strength, ability, activity, soldiers, company, goods, host, might, power, riches, strength, strong, substance, valiant, war worthy. This is who we are!

Let's change old perceptions and false ideologies about ourselves. Let's daily wear the identity of Chayil. Let's submit to Holy Spirit and allow His vision of us to rise to the forefront of our lives. Allow the identity of Chayil to be front and center.

This Chayil identity will have an effect on every area of our live. The Spirit of God lives inside of us. He will:

- ∞ Unlock force!

- ∞ Unlock wealth!

- ∞ Unlock strength!

- ∞ Unlock glory!

- ∞ Unlock favor!

- ∞ Unlocking power!

- ∞ Unlock riches!

- ∞ Unlock vision!

- ∞ Unlock ability!!

- ∞ Unlock destiny!

- ∞ Unlock His identity!

Here are some verses that affirm our beauty, our value and our true identity in Christ. Let the truth of His word bring us into a new place, to a new vision and to all we are created to be. I encourage you to say these words out loud - God sees me as beautiful and valuable!

Song of Solomon 4:7 NIV
"You are altogether beautiful, my darling; there is no flaw in you."

Psalm 139:13-14 NLT
"You made all the delicate, inner parts of my body and knit me together in my mother's womb.

Thank you for making me so wonderfully complex. Your workmanship is marvelous – how well I know it."

Ephesians 2:10
"For we are God's masterpiece, created do good works which God prepared in advance for us to do."

1 Peter 2:9
"You are a chosen generation, a royal priesthood, a holy nation, His own special people, that you may proclaim the praises of Him who called you out of darkness into His marvelous light;"

Ephesians 4:24
"And to put on the new self, created after the likeness of God in true righteousness and holiness."

Your Chayil Affirmation:
My identity is in Christ. I am who He says I am.
I am a Chayil woman.

ଔଓ

- Chapter Two -

THE VIRTUE OF CHRIST

Virtue means intrinsic excellence. Virtue is the word Chayil. It also means:

- ଔଓ Goodness
- ଔଓ Righteousness
- ଔଓ Integrity
- ଔଓ Dignity
- ଔଓ Honor

Someone with high moral principles - high moral ethics.

Philippians 4:8
"Finally, brethren, whatsoever things are true, whatsoever things are honest, whatsoever things are just, whatsoever things are pure, whatsoever things are lovely, whatsoever things are of good report; if there be any virtue, and if there be any praise, think on these things."

The Bible says we are to think on these things, meaning to take an inventory. We are to take an inventory of the things we think about and to make sure that virtue is included in our thoughts.

The second part of Proverbs 31:26 says that, "Her price is far above rubies." This means that your price - your value is more precious than any ruby, any pearl, any jewel.

I think to fully understand this, we need a better understanding of how much rubies are worth so we can really comprehend how much a Chayil woman is worth.

Reference to rubies are found in the King James Bible six times. The worth of rubies has diminished over the last couple of centuries but they must have been of serious worth in Biblical times.

Usually, when we think of valuable things in the terms of material worth, we think of gold or diamonds. However, if you ask a jeweler how rubies compare to diamonds and gold, you might be surprised to find out that rubies are rarer than diamonds, and considered of a higher worth. The best one-carat ruby cost eight times more than a one-carat diamond of the same quality!

Rubies are pinkish and or red in color. The brightest and most valuable shade of red is called blood-red. So we are blood red Chayil women purchased with the precious blood of Jesus.

> *1 Peter 1:9-10*
> *"For you know that it was not with perishable things such as silver or gold that you were redeemed from the empty way of life you inherited from your forefathers, but with the precious, valuable blood of Christ, a lamb without blemish or spot."*

This is our call to holiness - our call to virtue as a Chayil woman whose value is more precious than rubies!

I want you to think of your worth - your value as a woman -

even how our society views women. We are powerful!

So powerful and valuable that the enemy works hard to try to diminish our value or even to stop us all together! Our enemy certainly does not want us to walk together in unity! We become a powerful weapon against his works of darkness.

   ಚಿ Think about the rise of the current "Me Too" movement.

   ಚಿ Think about how we compare ourselves with other women.

The enemy wants us to be jealous of each other - not liking each other - finding fault with each other, not speaking to each other.

   ಚಿ How about the lies the enemy tells us about ourselves?

   ಚಿ How about lies we begin to believe or the lies we tell ourselves?

   ಚಿ How many women right now believe they are of little or no worth?

   ಚಿ How many societies, cultures, and religions still treat their women as property?

   ಚಿ How much do you value yourself and how much do you value the women in your life?

There are many women in your sphere and many women around the world who can benefit by knowing that they are blood red Chayil women, bought with a price, whose value is far above rubies!

Women need to know - they need to hear how much worth

they have, and how much God truly loves them.

Women are not sex symbols, property, slaves, or inferior humans.

As God made each part of creation, He said it is very good. Then God made Adam, and again, He said it is very good but I can do better so He made Eve!

As you are reading this, you are being charged to see yourself in a new way - through the loving eyes of your Creator. You are also being changed so you can see other ladies through the eyes of Christ. Tell the ladies in your life how much they are valued.

Tell those who believe they have no worth, because society tells them that they have no worth. Let them know its a lie!

Ask yourself:

> ❧ Do you feel worthless?

> ❧ Do you feel like you have no real value?

> ❧ Do you feel like what you do has no value?

Women wear so many hats. Some women work all day, then come home to even more challenges and it seems like they can be on a wheel that never stops turning!

Sometimes, it can feel like there is no value, or no worth to what women do.

Many women suffer from rejection - rejection from other women, rejection from men. They they try to put God in that same category.

But God is NOT like people. He is all together OTHER than we are!

People may let you down, but God never will. People may leave you, but God never will. People may lie to you, but God is the God of truth. He cannot lie!

Know that each of us is valuable to God and what we do has worth to God!

If there is any ounce of discouragement in you, stand up straight, blow the dust off your dreams, keep your focus on God and know that you are valuable!

If there is any ounce of discouragement in anyone you know, call them and tell them to stand up straight, blow the dust off their dreams, keep their focus on God and know that they are valuable!

We are a Chayil force! We are a Chayil army! We are wealthy! We are virtuous! We are Chayil women!

Our mandate is to empower ourselves, then go and empower someone else!

As a Chayil, virtuous women, you have a voice!

It is the enemy who tries to make you think you are not valuable. He tries to remind you of all the mistakes you have made.

Listen - If God does not remember or bring up your past, why do you remember it or bring it up? Why allow the enemy or another person to even try to bring up your past? We live today and we move forward in now revelation.

It is not wise to live in the past.

Every generation is looking to be served by those who carry God's heart.

We are part of an epic battle, but we have already won! So if you find yourself in warfare, remember that the attacks on your life have much more to do with who you will be in the future than who you have been in the past.

No one launches a large-scale, systematic assault against something or someone who is not considered to be a threat.

But it's not really about you. In fact, it really is not even your battle. The battle belongs to the Lord and He has already won!

We are his Chayil weapons of light in a world of darkness and it is our mandate to serve others in the dispensation of the times in which we live.

Know that we are daughters of the eternal Most High God - Jehovah Chayil - our Strength .....so we can live virtuously and brilliantly, and be intentional about enhancing the lives of others.

From this day forth -

- ৪০ Make no excuses for who you are.
- ৪০ You have a voice. People are waiting for you, not me, you.
- ৪০ Rule your world!
- ৪০ You are powerful, that's what God says about you!
- ৪০ You were created in the image of God with His

DNA and His likeness. You were created as a virtuous women who is well able to rule her world.

He gave us dominion so He makes all things unlimited in our lives.

Where we go, He is there. We Host the glory of God. Believe that you are who He says you are. You are a virtuous Chayil woman, destined to be blessed.

Your Chayil Affirmation:
The virtue of Christ is in me
and my price is far above rubies!

~ Chapter Three ~

THE VIRTUE OF FORCE

The meanings of the word Chayil are many! Since it gives us a picture of how God sees us, let's take a look at some of the meanings of Chayil.

A force is defined as the powerful effect felt by an organized body of military personnel or soldiers. Also, a group of people brought together for a particular activity.

- ಌ Force is also defined as:

- ಌ Power that causes an object to move.

- ಌ A strong influence.

- ಌ An organized and trained military group.

- ಌ A group of people who do the same job, or join forces with another person or group.

- ಌ A person with power to make something happen without offering the possibility of a choice.

When we know that the force of Jehovah Chayil lives in us, we become those who make things happen without offering the possibility of a choice.

My husband and I had a wonderful weekend visiting our daughter in college. We went to the airport to catch our flight to return home. The ticket agent reported bad weather in the area and stated that the flight would more than likely need to be canceled. That was not an option for us. We were scheduled to leave the next day on an international ministry trip so we needed to get home.

The Chayil force inside of me began to rise up. I spoke to my husband and told him that the Chayil force in me was not going to allow this flight to be canceled. We called on Jehovah Chayil - the One who make things happen without offering the possibility of a choice.

Shortly after we release the Chayil force, the ticket agent reported that the weather had turned in another direction. The Chayil force had triumphed! We were able to board our flight, make it home and prepare for our upcoming trip.

On another occasion, I had to take care of some business for my parents at a government office. As you may well know, lines in government offices can be very long!

I had an upcoming trip and my flight left later that afternoon. When I arrived, I was instructed to take a number from the machine. I noticed that they number they had just called was far from the number I had just taken.

I began to pray. The Chayil force in me called on Jehovah Chayil to move the numbers quickly on my behalf. The agents began skipping numbers. My business was taken care of and I was out of there in no time. The Chayil force had triumphed once again! I was able to make my flight in plenty of time.

In both of these examples, I was faced with the choice we are faced with each day. I could choose to either submit to the circumstances that presented themselves and let them control me or I could choose to allow the identity of Chayil force to rise up in me, partner with Jehovah Chayil and not offer the possibility of a choice.

No longer are we to just take what happens. With the identity of Chayil, we can create what happens.

> *Matthew 11:12*
> *"And from the days of John the Baptist until now the Kingdom of Heaven suffers violence, and the violent take it by force."*

The words of Jesus from Luke 10:17-19
> *"I saw Satan fall like lightning from heaven."*

I have given you the authority to trample on snakes and scorpions and to overcome all the power of the enemy; nothing will harm you."

When we read things such as:

- ❧ "Trample on snakes and scorpions."

- ❧ "Overcome all the power of the enemy."

- ❧ "Wage war."

- ❧ "Demolish strongholds."

- ❧ "Stand your ground."

We should understand that to go against Satan and his kingdom will demand the meeting of violence with violence and force with force.

The enemy is not afraid to use violence or force against us.

Let's not be afraid to be violent in worship.

- ঙ Violent in obedience.

- ঙ Violent in prayer.

- ঙ Violent in love.

- ঙ Violent in giving..

- ঙ Violent in the things of God.

It's time to be the Chayil force and to take the kingdom by force

It is the violent forcer who will seize the kingdom and take it by Chayil force.

Be a Chayil force to be reckoned with. That means you are strong and cannot be ignored. It means you are powerful - difficult to defeat!

Your Chayil Affirmation:
The force of Christ is in me. I am a Chayil force!

~ Chapter Four ~

THE VIRTUE OF CHRIST'S ARMY

The word Chayil also means an army. An army is a large organized body of armed personnel trained for war, especially on land. Why is warfare on land necessary? It is necessary because we have been given the assignment to dominate the earth. That is the mandate we were given in Genesis 1:26.

> *"God made us in His image and told us to have dominion over the fish of the sea, and over the fowl of the air, and over the cattle, and over all the earth, and over every creeping thing that creepeth upon the earth."*

Genesis 1:28 tells us to be fruitful, and multiply, and replenish the earth, and subdue it. We are assigned to bring it under subjection to the rule of God.

When we look in the word of God, we see that an army means a large number of persons organized for war. But the weapons of our warfare are not carnal!

> *2 Corinthians 10:4*
> *"For the weapons of our warfare are not carnal, but mighty through God to the pulling down of strong holds…"*

So our weapons of war are not carnal but they are mighty and they will pull down strongholds!

> *Ephesians 6:12*
> *"For we do not wrestle against flesh and blood, but against the rulers, against the authorities, against the cosmic powers over this present darkness, against the spiritual forces of evil in the heavenly places."*

> *Joel 2:25-29*
> *"And I will restore to you the years that the locust hath eaten, the cankerworm, and the caterpiller, and the palmerworm, my great army (Chayil) which I sent among you.*
>
> *And ye shall eat in plenty, and be satisfied, and praise the name of the LORD your God, that hath dealt wondrously with you: and my people shall never be ashamed.*
>
> *And ye shall know that I am in the midst of Israel, and that I am the LORD your God, and none else: and my people shall never be ashamed.*
>
> *And it shall come to pass afterward, that I will pour out my spirit upon all flesh; and your sons and your daughters shall prophesy, your old men shall dream dreams, your young men shall see visions:*
>
> *And also upon the servants and upon the handmaids in those days will I pour out my spirit."*

As the Chayil army of God, we must arise and stand strong. Jesus has won the victory, but we are here to enforce the victory He has won for us. This is a battle that only the church can fight. Governments cannot do it for us. We are the only ones who have been give the spiritual weaponry that's needed.

The Lord Jesus is our commander and the word of God is our guide. In an army, although there are different tasks and assignments, we all need each other to be in place in order to win the battle.

God is raising up an army of women who will for forward in power, defeat the enemies of righteousness and march forth in a victory procession! We have been called to be part of this army. We cannot march forward in fear.

Chayil army arise and be filled with the Spirit of God! We are a strong army and God is raising up a strong army of women around the globe!

> *Psalm 18:34*
> *"He trains my hands for battle."*

An army is also a mass of people organized for war. It can also mean a campaign or worship.

The word Chayil is used as army more times in the Word of God than any other word. Let the Chayil army arise and be filled with the Spirit of God!

> *Daniel 11:32B*
> *"...but the people that do know their God shall be strong, and do exploits."*

Those who know their God will display strength and take action without fear like a mighty army! Let's be the army of the Lord who joins forces to establish and advance His kingdom! We will change lives, one Chayil woman at a time.

We are his Chayil army!

Your Chayil Affirmation:
I am part of the Chayil army of God.

ଛ

~ Chapter Five ~

THE VIRTUE OF WEALTH

Chayil also means wealth! Wealth is defined as an an abundance of valuable possessions, money or resources. There are ten references in the Word of God where wealth is the word Chayil! Let's look at a couple of them.

Chayil is first mentioned as wealth in Genesis 34:29. It speaks of the time that Jacob's sons took the wealth (Chayil) of their enemies.

> *Proverbs 13:22*
> *"A good man leaveth an inheritance to his children's children: and the wealth (Chayil) of the sinner is laid up for the just."*

> *Deuteronomy 8:18*
> *"But thou shalt remember the LORD thy God: for it is he that giveth thee power to get wealth, that he may establish his covenant which he sware unto thy fathers, as it is this day."*

Go back and read all of chapter 8. Basically it says, when you increase, don't think it was your own hand that got you all the wealth.

Remember the Lord thy God! He is he one who gives you the power to get the wealth and then it says the reason for the wealth coming to you is so you can establish His covenant.

This is one area where the enemy has kept the church in a place of bondage.

> *3 John 1:2*
> *"Beloved, I wish above all things that thou mayest prosper and be in health, even as thy soul prospereth."*

We must believe what the word says about us!

To prosper means to succeed in your business affairs! I wish above ALL THINGS that you succeed!

God does not want us to trust in wealth, but God does want us to succeed!

> *1 Chronicles 29:11-12*
> *"Thine, O LORD, is the greatness, and the power, and the glory, and the victory, and the majesty: for all that is in the heaven and in the earth is thine; thine is the kingdom, O LORD, and thou art exalted as head above all."*

Both riches and honour come of thee, and thou reignest over all; and in thine hand is power and might; and in thine hand it is to make great, and to give strength unto all."

Riches and honor comes from God. In His hand it is to make great and to give strength to all. All means you and me.

> *1 Peter 2:9*
> *"But ye are a chosen generation, a royal priesthood, an holy nation, a peculiar people; that ye should shew forth*

the praises of him who hath called you out of darkness into his marvellous light:"

Let's start acting like the royal children of God that He has called us to be. You don't ever have to remind royals that they are royal. They grow up knowing who they are.

There are certain places a royal will not go. There are certain things a royal will not say. There are certain privileges that royals know and expect daily simply because they are royals.

If you are a single woman, do not settle for less than what you desire. Wait for your Boaz. Ruth 2:1 says Boaz was a "mighty man of wealth." Wealth is the word Chayil. Boaz was a Chayil man! That is the kind of man you want to find you!

Remember when God delivered the children of Israel from all those years in bondage to Pharaoh?

> *Exodus 12:35-36*
> *"And the children of Israel did according to the word of Moses; and they borrowed of the Egyptians jewels of silver, and jewels of gold, and raiment:*
>
> *And the LORD gave the people favour in the sight of the Egyptians, so that they lent unto them such things as they required. And they spoiled the Egyptians."*

In other words, when they left Egypt, they stripped them of their goods. Egypt is a type of the world.

> *Psalm 105:37*
> *"The LORD brought his people out of Egypt, loaded with silver and gold; and not one among the tribes of Israel was even feeble."*

Jeremiah 29:11
"For I know the thoughts that I think toward you, saith the LORD, thoughts of peace, and not of evil, to give you an expected end."

The word peace is the word shalom. Shalom means safe, well, happy, friendly, good health, prosperity, favor and peace.

God's thoughts toward you and me have an expected end, meaning the reward of that which you have longed for.

God's thoughts to the Chayil woman are thoughts of prosperity. Let's believe, receive it and enjoy the blessings of our King!

Your Chayil Affirmation:
My wealth is in Christ! He is my Shalom.

~ Chapter Six ~

THE VIRTUE OF WEALTH PART
2

I met a gentleman who had been a drug addict before he met Jesus and gave his heart to the Lord. He had some experience in accounting so he got a job working for an airline. He was so excellent at what he did that when promotion time came, the owner rewarded him by giving him the entire airline! This is a true story!

There are spheres of influence in our world that mold minds and control nations.

Unfortunately, the church has fallen under such a diluted form of Christianity that we have very little if any control in these spheres of influence.

World rulers of darkness operate through people in these spheres of influence. Their goal is to penetrate key strategic positions in leadership, and to populate these positions with people who will become gatekeepers to their ungodly agendas.

God wants His kingdom people at the heads of each sphere of influence. He wants His kingdom people in charge of companies and corporations.

We are called to change our sphere of influence. If this level of leadership power is our destiny, we are going to have to shift our thinking.

God wants this level of ruling power for kingdom leadership to operate in His people.

It has nothing to do with your culture, your background or your color.

The Bible tells us in Matthew 9 that it will be accomplished according to our faith!

> *Matthew 9:29b*
> *"...According to your faith be it unto you."*

    ℠ It is time for a paradigm shift in thinking!

    ℠ It is time out for I don't have or I can't do.

God wants us to be solutions. He want us to be those who lead and bring change to every area of society. We see that with the Proverbs 31 Chayil woman.

It is clear that she was a good steward of everything God placed in her hands.

How are we taking care of what God left under our control?

We know that we are stewards of all that belongs to God.

Stewardship is actually an Old English concept drawn from the days of castles and realms and the people who ran them. In those days people lived in realms—areas of land approximately the size of three countries.

In the middle of that realm was a castle, where the lord of the realm lived. The lord owned everything in the realm.

He owned all the land, all the farms, all the buildings, and all the commerce. Everything was under his control and authority.

The lord's castle was the nicest home in the realm, but there was another very nice house nearby. That's where the lord's steward lived.

The steward didn't own anything, but he took care of everything that belonged to the lord.

The steward managed the crop rotations, the labor force, the taxes, the banking, the commerce, and any of the lord's other interests.

That's what stewardship was all about—managing assets of the Lord. In essence, we are assets managers. We manage the investments of the King!

When we understand our responsibility as asset managers, we can receive what God gives us and enjoy what He has entrusted to us.

God is the Lord.

Psalm 24:1
"The earth is the Lord's and the fulness thereof." He owns it all. But we are responsible to manage His things for His glory.

Psalm 115:16
"The heaven, even the heavens, are the LORD'S: but the earth hath he given to the children of men."

That makes us stewards or managers of His resources.

Just like the Old English lord held the steward responsible for his stewardship, we are going to give an account of how we manage God's resources.

> *1 Corinthians 4:2*
> *"Moreover, it is required in stewards, that a man be found faithful."*

According to the Strong's Concordance, a steward is a house-distributor, a manager or overseer, i.e. an employee in that capacity, a fiscal agent, a treasurer, a preacher of the Gospel, a governor.

Regardless of our social status or bank account, the principles of biblical stewardship don't change.

We are managers of the mysteries of God as well as managers of all that belongs to God's.

He owns it all, so we can't hold anything in our hands tightly. If we're going to reclaim the biblical definition of stewardship and walk in the power of Chayil wealth, we have to make sure we understand God's ownership and our stewardship.

We have to embrace a paradigm shift that changes our thinking.

We must know that He owns everything and we own nothing.

- Our job

- Our house

- Our car

- Our family

෫ Our time

෫ Our money

All of these things belong to God.

If we stop thinking of ourselves as owners, it becomes much easier for us to open our hands (and our hearts) to use His money for His purposes.

Let's stop thinking like owners and start acting like managers.

Also, let's move from consumer mentality to producer mentality. Consumers want to have everything. Sometimes we just have too many things. As wealth producers, we want to multiply, give and meet the needs of others.

God is shaking us out of old paradigms

Chayil producers want to be a blessing to others and to equip people.

We must be Chayil wealth producers for the purpose of wealth distribution.

Let's read about the Chayil woman.

> *Proverbs 31:13-17*
> *"She seeketh wool, and flax, and worketh willingly with her hands.*
>
> *She is like the merchants' ships; she bringeth her food from afar.*
>
> *She riseth also while it is yet night, and giveth meat to her household, and a portion to her maidens.*

She considereth a field, and buyeth it: with the fruit of her hands she planteth a vineyard."

Proverbs 31:18-22
"She perceiveth that her merchandise is good: her candle goeth not out by night.

She layeth her hands to the spindle, and her hands hold the distaff.

She stretcheth out her hand to the poor; yea, she reacheth forth her hands to the needy.

She is not afraid of the snow for her household: for all her household are clothed with scarlet.

She maketh herself coverings of tapestry; her clothing is silk and purple."

Proverbs 31:24
"She maketh fine linen, and selleth it; and delivers belts unto the merchant."

Proverbs 31:27
"She looketh well to the ways of her household, and eateth not the bread of idleness."

Remember Deuteronomy 8:18
"But thou shalt remember the LORD thy God: for it is he that giveth thee power to get wealth, (Chayil) that he may establish his covenant which he sware unto thy fathers, as it is this day."

God is looking for asset managers. Say, "Here I am Lord. You - can trust me! Give me power to get wealth! I will carefully manage what belongs to you!"

I heard about a church in South Africa who built the first mall in their city. They did such an excellent job, that the government wanted to give them more land. That is Chayil wealth!

As Chayil women, we are destined to oversee multiple businesses. We are destined to be wealth developers for wealth distribution for kingdom advancement.

Remember, when presented with the promise land, many saw themselves as grasshoppers next to the giants. Only two people, Joshua and Caleb, dared to have faith and believe God. They said, "Let us go up at once. We are well able to take this land."

If you only see your current provision, it could keep you from seeing the complete, God-given vision.

Let's not be satisfied with just having a job. Instead, let's create and own a business or multiple businesses. Let's create multiple streams of income.

Don't be stuck in the world's system. Create your own system according to the Word of God.

- ࿔ Own lands!

- ࿔ Start businesses!

- ࿔ Own homes!

- ࿔ Buy cars!

- ࿔ Get into positions of rulership!

- ࿔ Don't think small. Dream big!

Ask God to show you what businesses He has for you.

No longer should we dance, shout, do church and have nothing.

In John 10:10, Jesus said He came to give us a super abundant life - life beyond measure. To have life more abundantly means to live a life that is superior in quality and abundant in quantity

Pray this prayer with me.

"Father, position me for the new opportunities you have for me. You can trust me to manage your assets!"

Your Chayil Affirmation:
I shall be a wealthy Chayil woman because
I am God's assets manager.

ა

~ Chapter Seven ~

THE VIRTUE OF WEALTH PART 3

As Chayil women, we are called to be solutions, not to just look for solutions. We are called to be wealth producers for the purpose of wealth distribution.

Remember the life of the Chayil woman.

> *Proverbs 31: 13*
> *"She keeps herself busy making wool and linen cloth."*

> *Proverbs 31:24*
> *"She makes clothes and belts, and sells them to merchants."*

This tells us that she makes things and sells them. She is a business woman.

> *Proverbs 31:16*
> *"She looks at land and buys it, and with money she has earns she plants a vineyard."*

She has vision for her finances.

> *Proverbs 31:17*
> *"She girds her loins with strength, and strengthens her arms."*

She is a hard worker, strong and industrious. She isn't lazy.

Proverbs 31:18-20
"She knows the value of everything she makes.

She spins her own thread and weaves her own cloth.

She is generous to the poor and needy."

She understands the value of her work and she is a giver.

In the chapter 6, we read about the steward. In order for the steward to manage the assets of the Lord, he would have had to have some keys that would have permitted him entry or access to everything that the Lord owned.

Matthew 16:18-19
"And I also say to you that you are Peter, and on this rock I will build my church and the gates of hell shall not prevail against it.

And I will give you the keys of the kingdom of heaven, and whatever you bind on earth will be bound in heaven, and whatever you loose on earth will be loosed in heaven."

In this passage of scripture, the word church is not a religious term and it does not refer to a building you or I may attend on Sunday. The Greek word for church is the word is ecclesia. It means those who are called out and it refers to the government of heaven on earth.

As the ecclesia, our privilege is to know the mind of the King, receive His thoughts, His desires, His passions and His intent and turn it into legislation that can be implemented for the Kingdom.

To be the ecclesia, those who are called out, we must stay in close contact with the King.

As His ecclesia, we have been trusted with information critical to the operation of the kingdom. This information is so critical that hell itself cannot prevail against the ecclesia.

God has given us keys to unlock the Kingdom, to take authority, to exercise dominion and to access all of heavens resources so we can legislate, manage and oversee the resources here in the earth realm.

Dr. Myles Munroe was a good friend and mentor to my husband and me. He taught us that keys represent authority, access, ownership, control, authorization and power.

I have no authority in your home, therefore, I do not have your keys. That means that I cannot access your home whenever I want to. However, if you as the owner of the home were to gives me your keys, I would have access to enter your home.

Dr. Munroe said "Keys cannot be substituted with feelings, emotions, wishful thinking or manipulation." If I stay outside of your home with the door locked, I could have an all night prayer meeting and cry all night but without the keys, the door will not open.

God has given us keys. These keys unlock the power and resources of the Kingdom. Dr. Munroe taught us that keys are principles. They are systems that operate under a fixed law.

   ઍ Keys are fixed laws – reliable standards that do not change.

   ઍ Keys activate function.

ຂວ Keys initiate action.

Jesus gave us the principles by which the Kingdom of Heaven operates. When used correctly, they work!

One of the keys to proper stewardship and asset management for increasing wealth is giving.

> *Luke 6:38*
> *"Give, and it shall be given unto you; good measure, pressed down, and shaken together, and running over, shall men give into your bosom. For with the same measure that ye give it shall be measured or given back to you."*

Why should we give? The Bible tells us in Genesis 8:22, "While the earth remains, seedtime and harvest or sowing and reaping."

ຂວ No seed, no harvest.

ຂວ No sowing, no reaping.

Sometimes we don't give because we let fear stop us. We are afraid that if we give, we may not have enough. Fear is connected to trust.

We must bind that spirit of fear and loose trust so we can use our key of giving as God tells us to and enter into a new measure of trusting Jehovah Jireh to provide everything we need.

Remember - it all belongs to the Lord. Nothing is ours.

The Lord owns everything, so everything that's under His control is also His responsibility. Giving is a key that we must use often and wisely.

Remember, Deuteronomy 8:18 tells us that it is God who gives us the power to get wealth!

God gives each of us the ability to yield wealth so He can establish His covenant.

The ability to get wealth is already in you! God put it there. It is called your intrinsic value. Intrinsic means that which belongs to a thing by its very nature.

It is that thing that is in you that is not in anyone else. It is your personal God key.

There are many people who play basketball well, but Michael Jordan was known to be the best. It may seem like a small thing just to put a ball in a hoop, but it gained him much notoriety and brought him much wealth. He played like no other. It was his intrinsic value. It was the key that he used that lead to increase and influence.

Colonel Sanders created a recipe for fried chicken. There just might be a recipe in your own kitchen for chicken that tastes a lot better but he had a vision that became his key that opened many doors and brought him into a place of increase and influence.

You have to believe in yourself and in the power of God who lives inside of you!

What is your intrinsic value? It is your key to your wealthy place. Your wealthy place is inside of you. What has God placed in you?

That is your key to unlock wealth. He gives each of us, you and me, the ability to get wealth.

- Can you cook? That could be your wealthy place.

- Can you sew? That could be your wealthy place.

- Can you talk? Perhaps that is your wealthy place!

Everybody has one! It is up to you to discover it and live in it!

Jeremiah 29:11 tells us that God knows the good plans that He has for us to give us a hope and a future. Ask God what His good plans are for you!

> *Ephesians 2:10*
> *"For we are his workmanship, created in Christ Jesus unto good works, which God hath before ordained that we should walk in them."*

You must know your intrinsic value because that is what empowers you and gives you authority.

What did God create you to do? You must find out so you can learn how to use your God key! Your God key will lead you to increase and influence.

It has been said that successful people do daily what normal people do occasionally.

"Ordinary people do occasionally, what unusual people do daily." Chayil women are unusual.

You must discover your wealthy passion, start doing it and don't let anyone else distract you from it.

Distractions come. You cannot stop them, but you can steward them. Do not accept anything not directly associated with your assignment.

Pay attention to what makes you smile - what makes you happy. What makes you sad? Those things may be clues to your wealthy place.

What would you do if money were no object? Write it down.

Begin to plan your work - then work your plan.

Use the keys the Lord has given you and begin to see your boundaries change.

Begin to look ahead to your next place of victory

- ∞ Declare the heavens open above you.
- ∞ Decree that you will see the heavens shift over your life

God has a new mantle for the new season. Receive it!

Part of this new mantle has to do with not living in the past relationships with wealth. Begin to see through spirit eyes - through eyes of faith.

God is not broke. He is your source. Your job is not your source so no more job mentality. Develop a Chayil mentality of business ownership

Today, decide to shift from consumer mentality to producer mentality.

- ∞ It's time to prosper.
- ∞ It is time to rule.
- ∞ It is time for wealth creation.

Let's become Chayil wealth producers for the purpose of

wealth distribution.

God gave Joseph an intrinsic value of wisdom. That was one of His God keys.

We can say the same for Esther, Deborah, Ruth, Mary and many more Chayil women of the Bible! They each had a unique quality that became their God key. As they were for their time, we are for now!

Chayil women - arise without compromise and without fear.

A greater measure of revelation, faith and overcoming grace to accomplish the assignment is being released to us today.

He who began the work in you is faithful and will complete it.

We empower ourselves, to empower others.

The transfer of wealth that has been prophesied is now ready for this season. No more delay, no more delay, no more delay.

This is the time and the season when we will see things we have not seen before in the people of God. God is ready to show up and show Himself strong on our behalf!

That which was prophesied shall now manifest! God Himself will fund the harvest.

    „ He will release creativity,

    „ He will release wealth in abundance,

    „ He is going to do it in ways that will shock us!

    „ He is going to turn hearts,

- He is going to release resource that have been held captive in people and in the nations.

- He will send His Spirit into the hidden places of the earth and uncover resources. No more delay!

This is the season we are in!

Darkness may abound in days ahead but there will be light for the sons of God.

God wants us to speak His word over our life! We are called to succeed and to fulfill His will in the earth. God does not want us to depend on our own skills or depend on man's wisdom.

God gave all of us His supernatural ability to order everything in our lives and when things come into divine order, His divine glory will manifest.

Your Chayil Affirmation:
There shall be no more delay in my life.
The wealth of Christ is in me.

છ

~ Chapter Eight ~

Your Chayil
WEALTH DECREE

First - Let's look at just a few Scriptures. You first have to believe that God wants to bless you!

We know Deuteronomy 8:18 says it is "God who gives us power to get wealth."

Wealth is the word Chayil.

He give each of us this power for wealth so that we can establish His covenant.

Write these scriptures down, speak them daily, study them and get them in your spirit. God watches over His work to perform it so speak the word daily over your life!

Genesis 12:2
"And I will make of <u>thee</u> a <u>great</u> <u>nation</u>, and I will <u>bless</u> thee, and <u>make</u> thy <u>name great</u>; and thou shalt be a <u>blessing.</u>"

In both of these verses, the word blessing is the word prosperity:

Blessing comes from the the word Barak. It means to kneel. It implies to bless God as an act of adoration or to abundantly thank Him.

Since we believe the word of God, we can worship and thank God even before we see the manifestation because we know His Word is true.

> *Psalm 115:14*
> *"The Lord shall increase you more and more, you and your children."*

> *Psalm 34:10*
> *"The lions may grow weak and hungry but those who seek the Lord lack no good thing."*

> *3 John 1:2*
> *"Beloved, I wish above all things that thou mayest prosper and be in health, even as thy soul prospers."*

> *Psalm 145:15*
> *"You open your hand and satisfy the desires of every living thing."*

> *Psalm 37:25*
> *"I have been young, and now am old; yet have I not seen the righteous forsaken, nor his seed begging bread."*

We have a key called obedience that unlocks many blessings.

> *Deuteronomy 28:6, 11-13*
> *"You will be blessed when you come in and blessed when you go out."*

The Lord will grant you abundant prosperity – in the fruit of your womb, the young of your livestock and the crops of your ground – in the land he swore to your ancestors to give you.

The Lord will open the heavens, the storehouse of his bounty, to send rain on your land in season and to bless all the work of your hands. You will lend to many nations but will borrow from none.

The Lord will make you the head, not the tail. If you pay attention to the commands of the Lord your God I give you this day and carefully follow them, you will always be at the top, never at the bottom."

In Malachi 3:10-12, God makes us a promise. "Bring the whole tithe into the storehouse, that there may be food in my house. Test me in this," says the Lord Almighty, "and see if I will not throw open the floodgates of heaven and pour out so much blessing that there will not be room enough to store it.

I will prevent pests from devouring your crops, and the vines in your fields will not drop their fruit before it is ripe," says the Lord Almighty.

Then all the nations will call you blessed, for yours will be a delightful land."

Deuteronomy 29:9
"Carefully follow the terms of this covenant, so that you may prosper in everything you do."

Proverbs 13:22
"A good person leaves an inheritance for their children's children, but a sinner's wealth (Chayil) is stored up for the righteous."

Matthew 6:33-34
"But seek first his kingdom and his righteousness, and all these things will be given to you as well. Therefore do not worry about tomorrow, for tomorrow will worry about itself."

Philippians 4:19
"And my God will supply every need of yours according to his riches in glory in Christ Jesus."

Psalm 66:12
"Thou hast caused men to ride over our heads; we went through fire and through water: but thou brought us out into a wealthy place."

A wealthy place is a place of satisfaction, a place of running over. It comes from a word that means to abundantly satisfy.

Psalm 112:1-3
"Praise the Lord. Blessed is the man that fears the Lord, that delights greatly in his commandments.

His seed shall be mighty upon earth: the generation of the upright shall be blessed.

Wealth and riches shall be in his house: and his righteousness endures forever."

Ecclesiastes 5:19
"Every man also to whom God hath given riches and wealth, and hath given him power to eat thereof, and to take his portion, and to rejoice in his labour; this is the gift of God."

Psalm 35:27
"Let them shout for joy, and be glad, that favor my

righteous cause: yea, let them say continually, Let the LORD be magnified, which hath pleasure in the prosperity of his servant."

Psalm 1:1-3
"Blessed is the man that walks not in the counsel of the ungodly, nor stands in the way of sinners, nor sits in the seat of the scornful.

But his delight is in the law of the LORD; and in his law doth he meditate day and night.

And he shall be like a tree planted by the rivers of water, that brings forth his fruit in his season; his leaf also shall not wither; and whatsoever he does shall prosper."

Genesis 39:2
"And the LORD was with Joseph, and he was a prosperous man..."

Joshua 1:8
"This book of the law shall not depart out of thy mouth; but thou shalt meditate therein day and night, that thou may observe to do according to all that is written therein: for then thou shall make thy way prosperous, and then thou shalt have good success."

In the book of Proverbs, wisdom is speaking.

Proverbs 3:16
"Length of days is in her right hand; and in her left hand, riches and honor."

Proverbs 8:18
"Riches and honor are with me; yea, durable riches and righteousness."

Proverbs 8:21
"That I may cause those that love me to inherit substance; and I will fill their treasures."

Proverbs 10:4
"He becomes poor that deals with a slack hand: but the hand of the diligent makes rich."

Proverbs 10:22
"The blessing of the LORD, it makes rich, and adds no sorrow with it."

Proverbs 22:4
"By humility and the fear of the LORD are riches, and honor, and life."

Our God is Jehovah Jireh. He is the God who sees our needs and provides.

Our God is Jehovah Shalom. Shalom means safe, well, happy, friendly, welfare, health, prosperity, peace, favor, good health, to be at rest, to have perfect peace. Shalom also means to prosper.

Psalm 122:6
"Pray for the peace of Jerusalem. They shall prosper that love thee."

God has a history of blessing His people! He blessed Abraham and made him extremely wealthy.

- ❧ He blessed Joseph and made him the prime minister of Egypt, with all the wealth and authority that go with that position.

- ❧ He blessed the children of Israel when they left

Egypt.

ဆ He blessed them again when He brought them into the promised land. He gave them houses they didn't build, vineyards they didn't plant, and wells they didn't dig.

ဆ He gave them gold, silver and spoils of war.

God is looking for a people He can trust with His wealth and wisdom so that they can have great influence on the earth for the Kingdom of God. He is looking for people to place in positions of authority so the light can overtake the darkness and His kingdom can be established in every sphere.

God wants us to be blessed so that we can be a blessing to others.

That is what He said to Abraham in Genesis 12:2: "I will make you into a great nation, and I will bless you; I will make your name great, and you will be a blessing."

Job 22:28
"Thou shalt also decree a thing, and it shall be established unto thee: and the light shall shine upon thy ways."

To decree means to cut down or off, to destroy, to divide, to exclude, or to decide. What shall we decree? To decree a thing means to decree a promise, or a word. It refers to something that was said. That which was said shall be accomplished. It shall be performed.

Isaiah 55:11
"So shall my word be that goeth forth out of my mouth: it shall not return unto me void, but it shall accomplish that which I please, and it shall prosper in the thing whereto I sent it."

Jesus said His words are "Spirit, and they are life." So when we take the Word of God into our mouth and say what He said, it becomes spirit and life.

The verse also says that when we decree, light shines upon our ways. That means we can see the way to go. Our path grows brighter and brighter.

This is our Chayil decree for wealth. Speak it out loud daily and make it personal.

In the name of Jesus, I decree the spirit of poverty to come off of me right now.

- Ω I decree that because I love you, you cause me to inherit substance and you will fill my treasures.

- Ω I decree that I will meditate in your word day and night and observe to do according to all that is written therein and I will make my way prosperous, and I will have good success.

- Ω I decree that because I fear your name and I delight greatly in your commandments, my seed shall be mighty upon the earth.

- Ω I decree that wealth and riches shall be in my house: and my righteousness endures forever.

- Ω I decree because it is written, the Lord shall increase me and my children more and more.

- Ω I decree that I will obey God's Word in every area of my finances, so He can prosper me.

- Ω I decree that I will bring all the tithes into the storehouse, and I will prove God in this. He said that He will open the windows of Heaven for me and pour me out such a blessing that there is not even room enough to receive it all.

    ဆ I decree that I am a good steward of God's blessings.

    ဆ I decree that as I seek wisdom, I will hear the Lord instructing me and teaching me in the way I should go.

    ဆ I decree that I am a doer of the Word, and not a hearer only.

    ဆ I decree that I will walk by faith and joyfully receive all God has for me.

    ဆ I decree that I will have a mentality of abundance.

    ဆ I decree that I will be a cheerful giver.

    ဆ I decree that my spirit, soul, and body are all open to receive the fullness of financial prosperity from the Father.

    ဆ I decree that my businesses will prosper, that I will have multiple streams of income, that I have favor everywhere you go, and that I am a radical and generous giver.

    ဆ I decree that I shall lend to many nations, but I shall not borrow.

    ဆ I decree that I have a heart of abundance and an attitude of expectation to receive my Father's blessings.

    ဆ I decree that the blessings of the Lord that makes us rich and adds no sorrow will come upon me and overtake me.

⁋ I decree that I open my mouth with wisdom and the law of kindness is on my tongue. Therefore, the fruit of my lips is blessed. .

Father, according to your Word, bless me and increase me. Let me increase exceedingly. Let me increase with the increase of God.

1 Chronicles 4:10
"Bless me indeed, and enlarge my coast. Let Your hand be with me, and keep me from evil."

Exodus 34:24
"Cast out my enemies, and enlarge my borders."

Deuteronomy 12:20
"Lord, You have promised to enlarge my borders."

I rejoice and I receive the blessings of God in my life!

Your Chayil Affirmation:
I am Chayil wealth and I decree that I will increase with the increase of God.

~ Chapter Nine ~

CHRIST'S VIRTUE
OF VALOR

Chayil also means valor. Valor means: Boldness or determination in facing great danger, especially in battle. Heroic courage or bravery. Fearless and bold - to be daring - to have backbone. Strength of mind or spirit that enables a person to encounter danger with firmness. Strength, especially on the battlefield or in the face of danger.

Valor is honor plus dignity.

Chayil women of valor are not passive. This is not the season to be passive! We are victorious, Chayil women of valor!

In Joshua chapter 1, we see the charge to valor. God was talking to Joshua but He is talking to us.

Joshua 1:1-10

"Now after the death of Moses the servant of the LORD it came to pass, that the LORD spake unto Joshua the son of Nun, Moses' minister, saying,

Moses servant is dead; now therefore arise, go over this Jordan, thou, and all this people, unto the land which I do give to them, even to the children of Israel.

Every place that the sole of your foot shall tread upon, that have I given unto you, as I said unto Moses.

There shall not any man be able to stand before thee all the days of thy life: as I was with Moses, so I will be with thee: I will not fail thee, nor forsake thee.

Be strong and of a good courage: for unto this people shalt thou divide for an inheritance the land, which I promised unto their fathers to give them.

Only be thou strong and very courageous, that thou mayest observe to do according to all the law, which Moses my servant commanded thee: turn not from it to the right hand or to the left, that thou mayest prosper whithersoever thou goest.

This book of the law shall not depart out of thy mouth; but thou shalt meditate therein day and night, that thou mayest observe to do according to all that is written therein: for then thou shalt make thy way prosperous, and then thou shalt have good success.

Have not I commanded thee? Be strong and of a good courage; be not afraid, neither be thou dismayed: for the LORD thy God is with thee whithersoever thou goest.

Then Joshua commanded the officers of the people, saying, Prepare you victuals; for within three days ye shall pass over this Jordan, to go in to possess the land, which the LORD your God giveth you to possess it.”

Joshua 1:14-18
“Your whole family can stay here in the land that was promised but you, tough soldiers (men of valor) must cross the River in battle formation, leading your brothers,

helping them;

Until God, your God, gives your brothers a place of rest just as he has done for you. They also will take possession of the land that God, your God, is giving them.

Then you will be free to return to your possession, given to you by Moses the servant of God, across the Jordan to the east.

They answered Joshua: "Everything you commanded us, we'll do. Wherever you send us, we'll go.

Then they encouraged each other by saying to each other, be strong and of good courage."

Many had put their trust in Moses to lead them but now there was a transfer of power taking place. The old familiar was no more. The new was there, whether they liked it or not.

Joshua had spent that time in the presence of God so when his time came to lead, he was ready!

They told Joshua that they would listen to him just like they had listened to Moses.

But he told them to be strong for their brothers also! Help them cross over so they can also inherit their promise!

Look at Judges 6:12. God gave Gideon an assignment that seemed impossible to him. He told him to go save his people! Then God sent an angel of the Lord to Gideon.

And the angel said to him, "The Lord is with you, O mighty man of valor."

Each of these references of valor are referring to men. What about the women? I know there are women who displayed this same quality.

Who came to my mind first? Deborah and Jael! Barak would not even go to war without Deborah!

Judges 4 tell us that Deborah was a judge in Israel and she called Barak to go to war and He said he would only go it she went with him. He would not go if Deborah would not go with him.

> *Judges 4:9*
> *"And she said, I will surely go with thee: notwithstanding the journey that thou takest shall not be for thine honour; for the LORD shall sell Sisera into the hand of a woman. And Deborah arose, and went with Barak to Kedesh."*

The Bible says there were 10,000 men...and Deborah! Sisera was the commander of Canaanite army. He brought all of his chariots to the battle .... 900 iron chariots in all!

Barak went after the chariots and all of Sisera's army died by the sword. There was no one left. Sisera got off his chariot and tried to flee on foot..

Sisera then went into the tent of Jael because he thought it was a place of peace. He told her he was thirsty so Jael invited him inside. The Bible says Jael gave Sisera some warm milk.

He asked her to tell anyone who may have been looking for him that he was not there. Of course, Jael agreed. Sisera had no idea that when he laid down to take a nap, that would be his last day on earth!

And while he was sleeping, a Chayil woman named Jael took

the future of her people into her own hands. She drove a tent peg through the head of Sisera. Twenty years of oppression ended because of one Chayil woman of valor with a tent peg in her hand.

Jael was a Chayil woman with boldness and determination who showed us what valor looks like when facing great danger, especially in battle.

She secured the destiny of her people. We also can lay hold of God's promises for our future! Rise up and drive the tent peg of the Word of God into the head of the enemies that try to rise up against you!

Chayil women of valor are not passive. This is not the season to be passive! It is time to be bold! We are to take the word of God in our mouth as a tent peg so we can see victory in every battle!

I don't know what kind of battle you might be facing today, but I do know that you can rise and use your tent peg and you will surely see the victory.

I release a spirit of valor on each of you as you read this and come into agreement with the Chayil attribute of valor! Rise up and make your decrees! Declare - "It is written..." That is how you use your tent peg!

- ৪০ Are you in a battle for the next generation? Decree that all your children will serve the Lord.

- ৪০ Are you in a battle for your health? Decree what the word says in Isaiah 53:5! You are healed "By His stripes."

- ৪০ Are you in a battle for your marriage? Decree what God has already declared. Say what is written in

Mark 10:9: "What God has joined together, let no man separate."

  › Are you in a battle with fear? It is written in 2 Timothy 1:7: "God has not given us a spirit of fear, but of power, love and sound mind."

  › Are you in a battle over your finances? Decree according to Philippians 4:19: "God shall supply all your needs according to His riches in glory by Christ Jesus."

We are victorious, Chayil women of valor!

Empower yourself, get your inheritance, then go empower someone else to become a woman of valor so she can also get what God has promised her!

Your Chayil Affirmation:
I am a woman with Chayil valor
because of the victorious One who lives in me!

~ Chapter Ten ~

CHRIST'S VIRTUE
OF STRENGTH

Chayil means strength. Strength means security, majesty, praise, boldness, might and power.

Proverbs 31:26
"Strength and honour are her clothing; and she shall rejoice in time to come."

Strength is what the Chayil woman wears. According to Psalm 18, we are girded with Chayil strength. David was a Chayil man.

1 Samuel 16:18:
"Then answered one of the servants, and said, Behold, I have seen a son of Jesse the Bethlehemite, that is cunning in playing, and a mighty valiant man (Chayil), and a man of war, and prudent in matters, and a comely person, and the LORD is with him."

Psalm 18:1-3
"A Psalm of David, the servant of the LORD, who spake unto the LORD the words of this song in the day that the LORD delivered him from the hand of all his enemies, and from the hand of Saul: And he said, I will love thee, O LORD, my strength.

The LORD is my rock, and my fortress, and my deliverer; my God, my strength, in whom I will trust; my buckler, and the horn of my salvation, and my high tower.

I will call upon the LORD, who is worthy to be praised: so shall I be saved from mine enemies."

Verse 6
"In my distress I called upon the LORD, and cried unto my God: he heard my voice out of his temple, and my cry came before him, even into his ears."

Verse 17
"He delivered me from my strong enemy, and from them which hated me: for they were too strong for me."

Verses 19-20
"He brought me forth also into a large place; he delivered me, because he delighted in me.

The LORD rewarded me according to my righteousness; according to the cleanness of my hands hath he recompensed me."

Verses 28-32
"For thou wilt light my candle: the LORD my God will enlighten my darkness.

For by thee I have run through a troop; and by my God have I leaped over a wall.

As for God, his way is perfect: the word of the LORD is tried: he is a buckler to all those that trust in him.

For who is God save the LORD? or who is a rock save our God?

It is God that girdeth me with (Chayil) strength, and maketh my way perfect."

Verse 39
"For thou hast girded me with strength (Chayil) unto the battle: thou hast subdued under me those that rose up against me."

To gird means to encircle as with a belt. It also means secure, to surround and to encompass.

King David goes on to say:

Verses 33-41
"He maketh my feet like hinds' feet, and setteth me upon my high places.

He teacheth my hands to war, so that a bow of steel is broken by mine arms.

Thou hast also given me the shield of thy salvation: and thy right hand hath holden me up, and thy gentleness hath made me great.

Thou hast enlarged my steps under me, that my feet did not slip.

I have pursued mine enemies, and overtaken them: neither did I turn again till they were consumed.

I have wounded them that they were not able to rise: they are fallen under my feet.

For thou hast girded me with strength unto the battle: thou hast subdued under me those that rose up against me.

Thou hast also given me the necks of mine enemies; that I might destroy them that hate me.

They cried, but there was none to save them: even unto the LORD, but he answered them not."

Verse 43
"Thou hast delivered me from the strivings of the people; and thou hast made me the head of the heathen: a people whom I have not known shall serve me."

Verses 46-49
"The LORD liveth; and blessed be my rock; and let the God of my salvation be exalted.

It is God that avengeth me, and subdueth the people under me.

He delivereth me from mine enemies: yea, thou lifts me up above those that rise up against me: thou hast delivered me from the violent man.

Therefore will I give thanks unto thee, O LORD, among the heathen, and sing praises unto thy name."

David is saying to God - You surrounded me with Chayil Strength and delivered me from all my enemies!

As God was with David, He is also with us. Chayil strength is in you. Chayil strength is in us!

Because God girds us with Chayil strength to fight our enemies, they have all been subdued under our feet. Therefore we are already delivered from all our enemies!

I have good news for you!

Psalm 84:6-7
"Who passing through the valley of Baca make it a well;
the rain also filleth the pools.

They go from strength to strength, every one of them in
Zion appeareth before God."

To pass through the valley of Baca means passing through the valley of weeping. If there has been a situation that has made you weep, God says I will cause you to go from Chayil strength to Chayil strength!

And the valley of weeping will become a place of springs where pools of blessing and refreshment collect after rains!

You will grow constantly in strength, and be invited to meet with the Lord in Zion. Chayil strength is found in the presence of the Lord!

Habaccuk 3:17-19a
"Although the fig tree shall not blossom, neither shall fruit
be in the vines; the labour of the olive shall fail, and the
fields shall yield no meat; the flock shall be cut off from
the fold, and there shall be no herd in the stalls:

Yet I will rejoice in the LORD, I will joy in the God of
my salvation.

The LORD God is my (Chayil) strength, and he will
make my feet like hinds' feet, and he will make me to
walk upon mine high places."

The Lord God is my Chayil! He makes me keep moving forward with confidence in Him knowing that His rule will prevail!

Be encouraged! He is your Chayil! He is your Chayil strength.

What is it that you need today? No matter what the situation is, fear not! Call on Jehovah Chayil!

Your Chayil Affirmation:
I am a strong Chayil woman
because Jehovah Chayil is my strength!

- Chapter Eleven -

THE VIRTUE OF CHRIST'S POWER

Chayil is power! Power means firm ability.

On the day that King David was delivered out of the hands of all of his enemies, he said:

> *2 Samuel 22:33*
> *"God is my strength and power: and he maketh my way perfect."*

Power is the word Chayil so David was declaring that God is his Chayil! It is His Chayil power makes our way perfect!

In Psalm 110:1-3 David wrote:
> *"The LORD said unto my Lord, Sit thou at my right hand, until I make thine enemies thy footstool.*
>
> *The LORD shall send the rod of thy strength out of Zion: rule thou in the midst of thine enemies.*
>
> *Thy people shall be willing in the day of thy power, in the beauties of holiness from the womb of the morning: thou hast the dew of thy youth."*

Power is the word Chayil. This is the day of His Chayil power!

This is the day for His Chayil worshipping warriors to arise.

Let's take a closer look at this text. Verse one says, "Sit thou at my right hand, until I make thine enemies thy footstool."

In biblical times, defeated enemies were brought back in chains and the victorious king would sit on his throne and put his feet on the backs of his defeated enemies as a sign of victory. Likewise, Jesus has conquered every enemy and has placed them put under His feet and under our feet.

Then He sat down in full authority!

Verse two says:
> "The LORD shall send the rod of thy strength out of Zion: rule thou in the midst of thine enemies."

The word rod is the Hebrew word Mattah. It means a ruling scepter.

It was a branch, as extending a rod. It was used for chastising, for throwing or for walking, like a staff.

The Mattah represents one's authority. The staff is first mentioned in Exodus 4:2, when God appears to Moses in the burning bush. God asks what Moses has in his hand, and Moses answered «A staff» or "A rod." The staff was then referred to as the "Rod of God" or the «Staff of God," which spoke of authority.

In Number 1:52, the Lord instructed Moses to have each of the 12 tribes set up their tent by divisions, each man in his own camp, under his own standard. So each tribe created their standards by taking a staff and carving the name of the tribe into the staff.

When a tribe would go into battle they would go out with their standard before them.

Psalm 110:2 tells us that He shall send the ruling scepter of His force, of His majesty - to tread down, to have dominion, to prevail against, to rule and to reign in the midst of His enemies.

I believe He is speaking about us! We have been sent into the earth to be the rod of His strength and to rule!

Verse 3 mentions His people, meaning a congregated unit, specifically a tribe or a troop - a nation of people, like the Chayil nation. They shall be willing in the day of His Chayil power.

Yes, power is the word Chayil! Here is what we are seeing.

After Jesus conquered sin and death and rose from the dead, He returned to the Father.

And the Father said, "Sit at My right hand, till I make Your enemies Your footstool."

So the throne attitude of Jesus is to sit. His defeated enemies were under His feet. As Chayil women, we need to develop a throne attitude. We have already won. We rule from our seated position, not from our earthly condition.

> *Colossians 2:15*
> *"And having spoiled principalities and powers, he made a shew of them openly, triumphing over them in it."*

> *Ephesians 1:20, 22–23*
> *"He raised Him from the dead and seated Him at His right hand…"*

"And God placed all things under His feet and appointed Him to be head over everything for the church, which is His body…"

We, the church, we are the body of Christ, and God Himself is telling us to have the same throne attitude as Jesus. We are to sit, while He makes our enemies our footstool.

All things, including the defeated enemies of disease, poverty, depression and all kinds of curses are under our feet.

Sitting implies resting. God wants us to rest from striving, rest from trying to figure it out on your own. He wants us to rest from our own labors. Let's enter into a place of rejoicing and praise. Let's rest in His finished work.

So we must know that our Chayil power comes from our position in Christ. No more crying over our condition - let's learn to rest and rule. Develop a Chayil throne attitude.

"Sit at my right hand…"

To sit at the right hand of an earthly king was a place of honor, a place of special trust and authority because of the relationship with the king.

It was something that was understood without needing explanation at the time. If you were to sit at the right hand of the King, it meant that you could act with his authority. Those who came to you would treat you with respect and obedience, as if you were the king himself.

Stay seated! Don't get up and try to handle things on your own!

The Chayil people of God shall be willing. The people of Israel went to Him as a nation, collectively, not as individuals.

They said to God, "We will do it. We will be willing."

Willing to do what? What were they willing to do? They were willing to voluntarily consecrate themselves for the service of the king.

What must we be willing to do? We must be willing to die to sin, willing to crucify the old man, in order that the new man, or Christ, may be formed in us. We must be willing to be weaned from our own thoughts and purposes, so the thoughts and purposes of God may be fulfilled in us.

When we are willing, God will beautify us with salvation, because there is nothing in us to hinder Him from working.

The willing ones will be wise, strong, powerful people, led by the Spirit of God who works in us to will and to do of His good pleasure - making us like Himself, to rule in the midst of our enemies.

Chayil people shall be willing while others are unwilling.

I am one of the "willing people"—are you?

- ➢ I am...

- ➢ ...willing to preach...

- ➢ ...willing to pray.

- ➢ ...willing to minister and serve others.

- ➢ ...willing to go to the prisons or the the nursing homes.

ↄ ...willing to go to prostitutes or to those less fortunate.

ↄ ...willing to go to the homeless.

ↄ ...willing to share the love of God and the message of Gospel anywhere, anytime.

ↄ ...willing to say here am I, send me!

The beauty of Christ is released through His willing ones. This is the day of His Chayil power!

This is the day for His Chayil worshipping warriors to arise to their rest, knowing we are already seated in heavenly places.

We must learn to rule from heavenly places, in order to rule in the midst of our enemies. No more wavering.

2 Timothy 2:4
"No man that warreth entangleth himself with the affairs of this life; that he may please him who hath chosen him to be a soldier."

Let's be done with low level thinking. Let's be done with low level warfare. Develop a Chayil throne attitude. You and I were created to rule in Chayil power. This is how we rule our world.

Your Chayil Affirmation:
I am a Chayil woman with a throne attitude.
This is the day of His Chayil power and I am willing!

~ Chapter Twelve ~

VALIANT -
A VIRTUE OF CHRIST

Chayil means to be valiant. Valiant means to be powerful, mighty and strong. To do valiantly is also the word Chayil.

> *Psalm 108:13*
> *"Through God we shall do valiantly: for he it is that shall tread down our enemies."*

> *Psalm 118:15b*
> *"The right hand of them Lord does valiantly (Chayil)."*

This says that the right hand of the Lord does Chayil! His right hand is filled with power and authority.

Let's look at three Psalms. The first is Psalm 60. This was a time when David was at war. He was actually in Babylon so he was a long way from home.

The prophets described Babylon as a city of pride and idolatry. The name Babylon means confusion. David was in a place of confusion. He was not in a good situation.

On the way home he fought with the Syrians. While this was happening, the Edomites, an old enemy of Israel, rose up and attacked Jerusalem.

David sent part of his army to fight the Edomites. But the Edomites beat them and killed 12,000 of his men. He wrote this psalm because he thought that the attack by the Edomites meant that God had left him and his people.

The Edomites must have broken the walls of some of the towns in Israel. The Psalm makes it sound like an earthquake might have taken place.

The Bible says the ground moved, and trees and buildings fell over. There were holes in the ground, and animals and people fell into them.

This was a difficult time. It was hard for David and his people to understand. Why did God let it happen?

How many times have things happened to us that we did not understand and we thought perhaps God was mad at us or maybe God had forsaken us and allowed the enemy have his way with us.

But God did answer them. Not only did He answer them, He sent them help. God is always faithful!

In essence, God was letting them know that everybody belongs to Him and He will decide what to do with them. He will even use our enemies for His work as He sees fit.

So David learned a lesson that all of us need to know. Vain is the help of man. Yes, God works through men and women to help us but only God can truly help us when we are in trouble.

Then David said something so powerful! No matter what it looks like, "through our God, we shall do valiantly."

Valiantly is the word Chayil! Thorough our Chayil God, we

shall do Chayil!

- ಐ We shall be a force!

- ಐ We shall prevail as an army!

- ಐ We have the ability to overcome!

Not only that, we shall tread down our enemies. We shall trample them under our feet. Through our God!

Then in Psalm 108, David repeats the same thing again! But Psalm 108 has to do with the end of exile! Many Jews had been prisoners-of-war in Babylon for 70 years.

At the end of that time the "new government" in Babylon let the Jewish people go back to their own country. They went back to build the city of Jerusalem again. They also built the temple, the house of God.

David is thanking God for giving him help to fight his enemies.

I love what He says here in Psalm 108:1-6.
"God, I have decided always to belong to you! I will sing your praise.

I will get up early and praise you.

LORD, I will thank you in front of all the people. I will sing your praises everywhere.

Your loving kindness is great. It is higher than the clouds.

Your truth reaches to the skies.

Use your right hand to answer us."

Then David repeats the words from Psalm 60 here in Psalm 108:12-13.

"Give to us help against the enemy, because help from men is of no value!

No matter what it looks like, through our God we shall do valiantly. With God we will beat everybody and walk all over our enemies."

Psalm 118 is about a whole nation in trouble. They cried, "Hosanna!" Which means save us now!

He had delivered the children of Israel from bondage in Egypt 900 years earlier and now He was set to deliver them again!

So they began by thanking God!

Psalm 118:1, 5
"Thank the LORD because He is good. His loving kindness will always be with us.

My enemy shut me in a prison. But I cried to the LORD. The LORD answered me and made me free.

The LORD is with me. I will not be afraid. What can anybody do to me?

The LORD is with me. He gives me help. So, I will see the LORD destroy my enemies."

Verse 8
"It is better to trust in the LORD than to trust in people."

Verse 10
"All the nations were round me like a cloud of bees, but I

destroyed them in the name of the LORD."

Verse 13-16
"My enemy pushed me so that I started to fall. But the LORD gave me help not to fall."

The LORD is my strength and my song and He is my salvation.

"The voice of rejoicing, shouting and triumph is in the tents of the righteous.

- ৯৩ The right hand of the LORD does valiantly (Chayil).

- ৯৩ The right hand of the LORD is exalted. The right hand of the Lord does valiantly (Chayil)."

- ৯৩ The right hand of the Lord does Chayil!

- ৯৩ The right hand of the Lord is force.

- ৯৩ The right hand of the Lord is ability.

- ৯৩ The right hand of the Lord represents God's ultimate power and authority. This is saying the right hand of the Lord brings forth Chayil power and Chayil victory!

- ৯৩ The right hand of the Lord executes Chayil!

- ৯৩ The right hand of the Lord accomplishes Chayil!

- ৯৩ The right hand of God is used throughout the Word of God as a symbol. The right hand of the Lord represents:

৯৩

- ∾ A symbol of power - Psalm 89:13

- ∾ A symbol of protection - Psalm 16:8

- ∾ A symbol of God's presence - Psalm 16:11

- ∾ A symbol of God's saving power - Psalm 60:5

- ∾ A symbol of victory - Psalm 18:35

- ∾ A symbol of the defeat of God's enemies - Exodus 15:6

- ∾ A symbol of God's mighty works - Psalm 45:4

- ∾ A symbol of judgment - Habaccuk 2:16

∾

- ∾ Jesus Christ is exalted to God's right hand - Hebrews 1:13

- ∾ Jesus Christ rules every authority at God's right hand - Ephesians 1:20-21

- ∾ Jesus Christ continues his work at God's right hand - Romans 8:34

- ∾ Jesus Christ will return at God's right hand - Matthew 26:64

- ∾ Jesus Christ takes a scroll from God's right hand. The scroll refers to God's decrees for the destiny of nations - Revelation 5:1-7

∾

The Bible also talks about the right hand of Jesus Christ.

∞ The place of the righteous on judgment day - Matthew 25:32

∞ A privileged place granted by the Father - Matthew 20:20-23

∞ A place of protection for Christians - Revelation 1:20

Jesus sits at the right hand of the Father and we are seated with Him. Take your seat!

We have been delivered from death, hell and the grave. We have been delivered from fear - from torment - from the lies of the enemy!

Psalm 118:17
"I will not die. I will live and declare and tell everyone what the LORD has done."

Let's say what David said in verses 28- 29:
"You are my God and I will praise you. You are my God and I will exalt you! I'll say that you are great.

Oh give thanks unto the LORD because he is good. And His mercy endures forever."

∞ The right hand of the Lord does valiantly!

∞ The right hand of the Lord is Chayil!

∞ The powerful hand of the Lord is Chayil!

∞ The victorious hand of the Lord is Chayil!

∞ The righteous hand of the Lord is Chayil!

∞ The mighty hand of the Lord is Chayil!

    ℴ The hand of His protection if Chayil!

    ℴ The hand of His authority is Chayil!

Through our God we shall do valiantly! We shall do Chayil! For it is He who will tread down our enemies!

Your Chayil Affirmation:
I am a Chayil woman and through my God
I shall do valiantly!

~ Chapter Thirteen ~

THE VIRTUE OF WAR

In some scriptures in the Word of God, the word Chayil is translated as war. War means to prevail in fighting a battle.

We know Jesus has already won the war for us but there are some battles we face from time to time. In any battle, we are Chayil strong - so we are always victorious.

In seasons of war, I believe God wants to show us how to take new ground.

He will give us warfare strategies that will cause our boundaries to increase for our future. In seasons of warfare, we must stay close to the Victor so He can show us how to shift into His divine order.

God often calls us to places we have not been before, but we must not fear the battle. We must not fear to go forward into new places.

In seasons of war, we cannot lose focus. If we do, we can become discouraged and go our own way. When we align ourselves with His plans and listen intently, He will set all things in order.

God has new alignments for us in days ahead. These new alignments will cause us to overtake every enemy!

He has already won the victory. We war to enforce the victory He has already won for us. We can live Chayil strong and in the power of my might.

In Jeremiah 51:20, God said to Israel, what He now says to us. "You are my hammer (my war club - my battle axe) and weapon of war: with you I break nations in pieces; with you I destroy kingdoms;"

He has called us to be strong, Chayil women. We strike down everything that is not like God so let's allow God to train our hands for war.

There are seasons when we must war to for our joy - war for our peace and war for our increase. We will not be defeated and we will take the spoils of each battle.

Let us cast off the armor that we have warred with in past seasons. That armor was used to win many battles. But that is not the armor that is necessary for us in the days ahead. God gives us new weapons for new wars.

In the midst of our wars, we will be clothed with strength and honor until we are wearing the garment of His triumphant bride.

These are garments with the victory of the land, not garments with the iniquities of the land.

Deuteronomy 3:18
"And I commanded you at that time, saying, The LORD your God hath given you this land to possess it: ye shall pass over armed before your brethren the children of

Israel, all that are meet for the (Chayil) war."

We have been given a command - a charge. We have been given the land to posses it - to occupy it.

To occupy means to drive out whoever is currently on the land God has promised us. It means to seize the land - to cast out, consume, destroy, disinherit, dispossess and drive out sickness, lack, fear, and depression.

We are going to pass over! This means we are going to go beyond where we are now. We will pass over armed and equipped for the fight! God has already given us what we need to win every battle!

2 Corinthians 10:3-6
"For though we walk in the flesh, we do not war after the flesh:"

(For the weapons of our warfare are not carnal, but mighty through God to the pulling down of strong holds;)

Casting down imaginations, and every high thing that exalts itself against the knowledge of God, and bringing into captivity every thought to the obedience of Christ;

And having in a readiness to revenge all disobedience, when your obedience is fulfilled."

The Greek word for warfare means strategies. The Kingdom is not for the faint of heart or for those looking for an easy road.

It is for those who are willing to do whatever is necessary to follow the charge of our King. We are often called to be on the offense!

We must press past the norm so we can pass over! We have already been equipped and God has given us the land to possess. What is the land you need to possess?

- ₭ What ministry has God told you to start?

- ₭ What book has He told you to write?

- ₭ What business has He told you to start?

Chayil woman, you are well able. Yes, you may have to war to step into your inheritance, but it is yours! Take it by force!

There is a shaking and a shifting taking place in the body of Christ.

There is a stirring in God's people, a discontent with church as usual. His call is for us to step out of mediocrity and into the fullness of His call.

In these last days, the resurrection, life giving power that was in the second Adam, Jesus Christ, will be seen in His sons.

God has called each of us by name at a strategic time in history. He has put you in a strategic place for His purposes.

It does not matter what has happened to you in the past. You are here right now! Each one of you is needed. Each one of you is important for the plan of God for your region.

Do not buy the lie that you are not needed. Remember, according to Ephesians 4:16, every joint of the body contributes.

We each have a prophetic destiny to fulfill and we need you do the part God has called you to do.

Chayil woman – arise!

This may be a season of war, but we have already won every battle.

We are shifting! The shift will take us from what we have known to what God knows. Let's expect higher, surrender higher and believe higher. Let's connect with people of like belief, like surrender and like faith. Let's connect with those willing to go to the same level of Chayil!

Your Chayil Affirmation:
I am a Chayil woman and every battle is already won.

~ Chapter Fourteen ~

The Virtue of WORSHIP

The root word of Chayil is to guwl, meaning to twist or whirl in a circular or spiral manner, specifically to dance. That tells us that worship is very important and a key ingredient to the life of a Chayil woman.

The word army also means to worship. There is a company of Chayil worshippers, ready and prepared to understand the power of our worship and how to use worship as a weapon of our warfare!

In Psalm 22: 3, we are told that God inhabits the praises of His people.

To inhabit our praises means that God builds His throne in the midst of our praise and worship. When He comes, the full weight of who He is comes! His presence is not for goosebumps. His presence assures our victory!

In the midst of our worship, God comes and we partner with Him to send His judgement against our enemies!

Read through the book of Revelation. You will see that in the midst of worship, God sent out His judgements against His enemies in the midst of worship.

Psalm 149:6-9:
"Let the high praises of God be in their mouth, and a
twoedged sword in their hand;

To execute vengeance upon the heathen, and punishments
upon the people;

To bind their kings with chains, and their nobles with
fetters of iron;

To execute upon them the judgment written: this honour
have all his saints. Praise ye the LORD."

The picture here is of a courtroom. In a courtroom, there is a judge.

When someone has committed a crime, they come before the judge. The judge renders a verdict and writes the judgement. The Bailiff is the one who executes the judgement that has been written by the judge. That is us! We are the Bailiff!

God is the judge of the whole earth. Satan is the enemy of our souls and has committed crimes against humanity. We are the Bailiff. We execute the judgement that has been written!

We say, "It is written.' We use our sword just as Jesus did when He was tempted in the wilderness. The Word of God is the judgement that has been written against every enemy.

According to the Psalm, our high praises executes vengeance, punishments, binds kings and executes God's written judgement.

That is why we need to know the word because the word is our sword and when we mix the word of God with the praises of God, we win every time!

Worship is a powerful key. Worship has to do with who will win the war for the territory.

My husband and I were attending a conference in Chicago, Illinois.

I was scheduled to speak at the morning service. I had heard that there was a political rally coming to the city. The rallies had been known to be places where violence could easily erupt.

I inquired of the Lord about the message He wanted me to bring forth. He told me to release His names over the region. We began to allow the high praises of God to be released, along with the names of God and the Word of God.

It would be a good testimony to say that there was no violence at the rally. God did even better than that. The rally was canceled! Glory to God!

We took control of the atmosphere through praise and worship. Only God knows whose life may have been spared because the rally was canceled.

Chayil worship is for more than goosebumps. Chayil worship is power! Be free to worship! Dance! Jump! Spin around! Bow down! Run! Leap for joy! Let the exalted shouts of God be in your mouth and a two-edged sword in your hand! Execute the judgment God has written. "This honour have all his saints. Praise ye the LORD."

Your Chayil Affirmation:
I am a free Chayil worshipper.
I change atmospheres because of His virtue in me.

ജ

~ Chapter Fifteen ~

WISDOM -
THE VIRTUE OF CHRIST

Proverbs 31:26
"She opens her mouth with wisdom and the law of
kindness of on her tongue."

I have a friend who is a Rabbi. He said that each letter of the
Hebrew alphabet has a numerical value. That means that
everyone's name is a number and we all have a scripture in the
Bible according to our name.

Guess what my bible scripture is! Proverbs 31:26. How about
that!!! That is that scripture that my name represents.

As Chayil women, we are to open our mouth with skillful and
godly wisdom and let the law of kindness be on our tongue.
We will discuss the law of kindness in the next chapter.

This means that as Chayil women we have control over what
we speak! We have control over what comes out of our
mouths!

According to Matthew 12:34-35:
    "...Out of the abundance of the heart, the mouth speaks.

    A good man out of the good treasure of the heart brings

forth good things: and an evil man out of the evil treasure brings forth evil things."

So we must have godly thoughts in our heart because we speak that which is in our heart, so our heart must first be yielded and submitted to God.

- ɞ When the Chayil woman speaks, she speaks with wisdom, with kindness and graciousness.

- ɞ When the Chayil woman speaks, she speaks things that will bless and benefit others and she speaks the truth in love.

- ɞ When the Chayil woman speaks, she gives godly counsel and instruction.

ɞ

- ɞ Chayil women do not waste time gossiping or complaining. Neither does she listen to others gossip and complaining.

- ɞ The Chayil woman is not manipulative, nor does she dwell on the negatives or feel sorry for herself.

- ɞ The Chayil woman does not meddle in low level warfare or entangle herself in the affairs of this life! But she enriches the lives of others.

- ɞ As Chayil women, what should we be saying when we open our mouths?

Matthew 17:20
"And Jesus said unto them......for verily I say unto you, If ye have faith as a grain of mustard seed, ye shall say...

unto this mountain, remove hence to yonder place; and it
shall remove; and nothing shall be impossible unto you."

Faith speaks!

Mark 11:22-23
".....have faith in God."

For verily I say unto you, That whosoever shall say..."

Whosoever shall say what?

"Say unto this mountain, Be thou removed, and be thou cast into the sea; and shall not doubt in his heart, but shall believe that those things which he saith shall come to pass; he shall have whatsoever he saith."

What mountains do you need to remove?

    „ Mountains of debt?

    „ Mountains of sickness?

    „ Mountains of resistance from the enemy?

What mountains do you need to speak to? In order to remove the mountains, you have to say something! Open your mouth with wisdom and remove it!

God's word is wisdom! Jesus has made unto us wisdom. So let's say what Jesus said! He said in John 6:63 that the words that He speaks, "...They are spirit and they are life."

As Chayil women, we speak words of life!

Words are one of the most important things in life and one of the most powerful weapons that we have. Jesus said,

"Whatsoever YOU say.' Not what I say to you, but what do YOU say? Are you speaking words of wisdom?

Listen to yourself when you speak. Remember Proverbs 18:21: "Death and life are in the power of your tongue and they that love it will eat the fruit thereof."

That means that words are also seeds that will produce the fruit of what you say. The life of your marriage - the future of your children - your destiny is in the power of your tongue.

The worlds were framed by words.

> *Hebrews 11:3*
> *"Through faith we understand that the worlds were framed by the word of God, so that things which are seen were not made of things which do appear."*

Everything you see today came about because of words. In the beginning, God said.....and there was. There is nothing that God said that did not come to pass.

In Genesis 1:11, when God said..." Let the earth bring forth grass", grass came forth. Tomatoes didn't come forth. Grass came forth.

He wants us to operate the same way. Chayil woman, be careful what you say. It will manifest

It first has to start with what you believe God for - what you use your key of faith for.

Words are keys. When mixed with faith, words will unlock doors.

You have to speak it, without doubting. Doubt cancels faith.

৪০ Choose your thoughts.

৪০ Choose your words.

৪০ Choose your life.

2 Corinthians 10:5:
"Bring every thought into captivity to the obedience of Christ..."

We have to make our thoughts obey God! Why?

Proverbs 23:7
"As a man thinks in his heart, so is he."

As a man thinks, meaning a continual process. Not as a man has thought one time. I encourage you to pay attention to your thoughts.

If we are not careful, our thoughts can lie to us and cause us to speak things that are not filled with the wisdom of God.

Remember, negative faith is still faith. It is powerful. It is faith that something bad will happen. This is what causes anxiety, worry, doubt and fear.

Negative faith can get into your heart and affect your words and you have what you say because what you say will manifest.

৪০ Choose your thoughts.

৪০ Choose your words.

৪০ Choose your life.

৪০

ဢ Change your thoughts.

ဢ Change your words.

ဢ Change your life.

Wisdom must be found in our thoughts, words and in our actions. So wisdom affects every part of our lives. When the Chayil woman speaks, wisdom is what must be released.

Hear the word of the Lord.

> *Psalm 141:3*
> *"Set a guard, O LORD, over my mouth; keep watch over the door of my lips."*
>
> *Proverbs 21:23*
> *"Whoever keeps his mouth and his tongue keeps himself out of trouble."*
>
> *Ephesians 4:29*
> *"Let no corrupting talk come out of your mouths, but only such as is good for building up others that it may give grace to those who hear."*
>
> *James 3:5*
> *"So also the tongue is a small member, yet it boasts of great things. How great a forest is set ablaze by such a small fire!"*
>
> *1 Peter 3:10*
> *"Whoever desires to love life and see good days, let him keep his tongue from evil and his lips from speaking deceit;"*
>
> *Psalm 19:14*
> *"Let the words of my mouth and the meditation of my*

heart be acceptable in your sight, O Lord, my rock and my redeemer."

James 1:19
"Know this, my beloved brothers: let every person be quick to hear, slow to speak, slow to anger;"

Proverbs 15:1
"A soft answer turns away wrath, but a harsh word stirs up anger."

Proverbs 25:11
"A word fitly spoken is like apples of gold in a setting of silver."

Proverbs 18:7
"A fool's mouth is his ruin, and his lips are a snare to his soul."

Proverbs 29:20
"Do you see a man who is hasty in his words? There is more hope for a fool than for him."

Psalm 49:3
"My mouth shall speak wisdom; the meditation of my heart shall be understanding."

Ladies. We are Chayil women! Let's not allow our mouth to get us into trouble!

Colossians 4:6 tell us that our speech should always be gracious and "seasoned with salt" so that we may know how to answer any one we speak to.

Proverbs 15:4 says that a gentle tongue has healing power and is a "tree of life."

Proverbs 12:18 says that the "tongue of the wise" brings healing.

Let us submit our hearts, our thoughts and our mouths to Holy Spirit. Let us wisely build others up with our mouths and not tear others down.

- &○ We are Chayil women whose hearts and minds are be filled with the Word of God so we can glorify God and be a blessing to those around us.

- &○ When a Chayil woman speaks, wisdom is released! Decree that you will open your mouth with wisdom!

Your Chayil Affirmation:
I am a Chayil woman.
Therefore, I always open my mouth with wisdom.

ജ

- Chapter Sixteen -

THE LAW OF KINDNESS
IS THE VIRTUE OF CHRIST

Proverbs 31:26
"She opens her mouth in skillful and godly wisdom and on her tongue is the law of kindness (giving counsel and instruction)."

One of the things that makes us Chayil women is that a Chayil woman has control over her mouth. Not only does she open her mouth with wisdom, but the law of kindness is on her tongue.

When a Chayil woman speaks, she speaks with kindness and graciousness. She speaks things that will bless and benefit others. She speaks the truth in love.

A Chayil woman does not dwell on the negatives. We do not have pity parties! We are women of faith and that is reflected in our speech! Out of the abundance of the heart, the mouth speaks. So let's let the fruit of kindness grow within our heart.

Colossians 3:12:
"Therefore, as the elect of God, holy and beloved, put on (or clothe yourself with) tender mercies, kindness, humility, meekness, long-suffering."

2 Peter 1:4-8
"Whereby are given unto us exceeding great and precious promises: that by these ye might be partakers of the divine nature, having escaped the corruption that is in the world through lust.

And beside this, giving all diligence, add to your faith virtue; and to virtue knowledge;

And to knowledge temperance; and to temperance patience; and to patience godliness;

And to godliness brotherly kindness; and to brotherly kindness charity.

For if these things be in you, and abound, they make you that ye shall neither be barren nor unfruitful in the knowledge of our Lord Jesus Christ."

Kindness is a law. How does man define the law?

1. A system of rules that a particular country or community recognizes as regulating the actions of its members and may enforce by the imposition of penalties.

2. A statement of fact, deduced from observation, to the effect that a particular natural or scientific phenomenon always occurs if certain conditions are present.

3. The body of divine commandments as expressed in the Bible.

The Bible defines law as a decree, a commandment - that which governs. It also means, to cut in stone. Once a law is cut in stone, it cannot be removed unless the stone is cut again.

When we speak words, we cannot take them back. It is the same thing as cutting or writing or making a decree in stone and the only thing that can remove it is to make another decree.

That is why our words are so important. Words are like governors. The words we speak will govern our lives.

Proverbs 18:21
"Death and life are in the power (ability) of the tongue and they that love it shall eat the fruit thereof."

I want to share something I read recently. The author told her story about how God taught her to pray for her daughter from the courts of heaven.

She shares how God showed her that the words she spoke about her daughter while her daughter was in a backslidden condition had actually contributed to holding her daughter captive.

She recalls saying things like, "She doesn't even see that she is in sin. She is totally blind to what is happening to her. She won't listen to anything we are saying to her."

So God showed her that she needed to repent of speaking these words because the words began to govern her daughters life.

She writes, "We may have forgotten words that we have spoken but the accuser has a record of them to present to the court."

Let's not only repent for the words we have spoken, but let's stand in the gap for others concerning negative things they may have said about us.

So kindness is a law and we will eat the fruit of kindness. Let's look a little closer at the law portion of this.

The book of Matthew lets us know that we are the church - we are the body of Christ.

As His Ecclesia, we are the ones called to stay in close contact with the King. We must know His heart, His mind and His desires so we can turn them into legislation in the earth.

To legislate means to perform the function of legislation, specifically to make or enact laws. It means to mandate, establish, or regulate by or as if by legislation.

In other words, we are legislators for the government of heaven. Next time someone asks you what you do, tell them you are a legislator!

Since God's word is His law, we legislate according to God's word. We legislate according what the King has already said.

I was having some pain in my legs. I began to legislate healing according to the Word of God and the pain left.

Recently, I was traveling on a plane. A child sitting near me began to cry. I had a decision to make. I could listen to the child cry or I could legislate peace to the child so everyone seated near the child could have a peaceful three hour flight.

I began to legislate as I sat in my seat. Within seconds, the child stopped crying and we all had a great flight.

Joshua 1:8
This book of the law shall not depart from your mouth, but you shall meditate in it day and night, that you may observe to do according to all that is written in it. For

then you will make your way prosperous, and then you will have good success.

It is a law of the kingdom that as long as we keep this law of God's word, meditate day and night and observe to do all that is written, we will make our way prosperous and have good success. It is a law that will govern our lives.

Just as God established physical laws, such as the law of gravity, so there are spiritual laws that have been set in motion by God. The spiritual laws are just as sure as physical laws.

God's physical laws can be found in a physics book. His spiritual laws can be found in the Word of God, the Bible.

Every day we get up and get out of bed and never think about the law of gravity but that law acts as a governor in our lives daily. It affects what we do regardless of whether we are thinking of it or not.

There are many natural laws, many spiritual laws and many laws mentioned in the word of God.

God and His kingdom operates under a set of strict spiritual laws.

Romans 3:27 mentions the law of faith. Faith is a spiritual law. Hebrews 10:38: ...The "just shall live by faith."

Romans 8:2
"The law of spirit of life in Christ Jesus has set me free from the law of sin and death."

Here we see two laws - life in Christ and sin which results in death.

It is a law. If you sin, you die. If you are in Christ, you live.

The law of life in Christ Jesus supersedes the law of sin and death.

So by being born again and embracing the law of the Spirit of Life in Christ Jesus, we overcome the law of sin and death.

Sowing and reaping is a natural law that farmers understand. They plant specific seeds to get specific crops and harvests. They do not plant corn seeds to get cabbage.

They understand that whatever they sow, is exactly what they reap.

This is a spiritual law as well as a natural physical law.

Galatians 6:7
"Be not deceived; God is not mocked: for whatsoever a man soweth, that shall he also reap."

He tells us clearly that this is a spiritual law that governs our lives. Sowing and reaping is a spiritual law. It affects everyone equally, whether they realize it or not.

So kindness is a law and it is the assignment of the ecclesia to legislate, to make laws, according to the word of God. What are you legislating? You have whatever you say. When we speak His word, we legislate so we can manifest that which has already been established by God.

Let's say you are in a situation that is contentious.

Proverbs 15:1
"A soft answer turns away wrath."

Empower yourself and empower others by allowing the law of kindness to be the words that you speak!

> *James 3:5-18*
> *"Likewise, the tongue is a small part of the body, but it makes great boasts. Consider what a great forest is set on fire by a small spark."*

The tongue also is a fire, a world of evil among the parts of the body. It corrupts the whole body, sets the whole course of one's life on fire, and is itself set on fire by hell.

All kinds of animals, birds, reptiles and sea creatures are being tamed and have been tamed by mankind, but no human being can tame the tongue. It is a restless evil, full of deadly poison.

With the tongue we praise our Lord and Father, and with it we curse human beings, who have been made in God's likeness.

Out of the same mouth come praise and cursing. My brothers and sisters, this should not be. Can both fresh water and salt water flow from the same spring?

My brothers and sisters, can a fig tree bear olives, or a grapevine bear figs? Neither can a salt spring produce fresh water.

Who is wise and understanding among you? Let them show it by their good life, by deeds done in the humility that comes from wisdom.

But if you harbor bitter envy and selfish ambition in your hearts, do not boast about it or deny the truth. Such wisdom does not come down from heaven but is earthly, unspiritual, demonic.

For where you have envy and selfish ambition, there you find disorder and every evil practice.

But the wisdom that comes from heaven is first of all pure; then peace-loving, considerate, submissive, full of mercy and good fruit, impartial and sincere.

Peacemakers who sow in peace reap a harvest of righteousness."

Paul wrote to the congregation and reminded them that no unwholesome talk should come from the mouth, but only words that will edify others.

Proverbs contain countless warnings about the danger of an unbridled tongue.

I read something that said only God can truly live the life of God so let's allow God to live His life through us - love through us - bless others through us - speak through us.

Chayil women, by the power of Holy Spirit, let's make our thoughts and tongue obey God.

Sometimes your best weapon is the law of kindness. Tame the tongue - you will eat the fruit thereof. Determine to speak according to the law of kindness.

Your Chayil Affirmation:
I am a Chayil woman.
I open my mouth with wisdom
and the law of kindness will always be on my tongue.

ॐ

~ Chapter Seventeen ~

THE VIRTUE OF
THE FEAR OF THE LORD

Proverbs 31:30
"Favor is deceitful, and beauty is vain: but a woman who fears the Lord, she shall be praised."

A Chayil woman is a woman who fears the Lord.

The Bible mentions two specific types of fear.

The first type is beneficial and is to be encouraged. The second type is a detriment and is to be overcome. The first type of fear is fear of the Lord.

This type of fear does not necessarily mean to be afraid of something. Rather, it is a reverential awe of God; a reverence for His power and glory.

However, it is also a proper respect for His wrath and anger. In other words, the fear of the Lord is a total acknowledgement of all that God is, which comes through knowing Him and His attributes.

Fear of the Lord brings with it many blessings and benefits.

Psalm 111:10 tells us that the "Fear of the Lord is the

beginning of wisdom" and leads to good understanding.

> *Proverbs 1:7*
> *"Only fools despise wisdom and discipline."*

Furthermore, fear of the Lord leads to life, rest, peace, and contentment (Proverbs 19:23).

It is the fountain of life (Proverbs 14:27) and provides a security and a place of safety for us (Proverbs 14:26).

However, the second type of fear mentioned in the Bible is not beneficial at all.

This is the "spirit of fear" mentioned in 2 Timothy 1:7: "For God has not given us a spirit of fear, but of power and of love and of a sound mind"

A spirit of fearfulness and timidity does not come from God.

However, the enemy tries to bring fear, sometimes this "spirit of fear" tries to overcome us, but to overcome it we need to trust in and love God completely.

> *I John 4:18*
> *"There is no fear in love. But perfect love drives out fear, because fear has to do with torment. The one who fears is not made perfect in love."*

All throughout the Bible, from the book of Genesis and continuing throughout the book of Revelation, God reminds us to "Fear not."

> *Isaiah 41:10*
> *"Do not fear, for I am with you; Do not anxiously look about you, for I am your God. I will strengthen you,*

surely I will help you, Surely I will uphold you with My
righteous right hand."

Often we fear the future and what will become of us. But Jesus reminds us that God cares for the birds of the air, so how much more will He provide for His children?

We are worth more than many sparrows (Matthew 10:31).

> *Psalm 56:11*
> *"In God I trust; I will not be afraid. What can man do*
> *to me?" This is an awesome testimony to the power of*
> *trusting in God.*

Once we have learned to put our trust in God, we will no longer be afraid of the things that come against us.

People are afraid or worried about so many things. But the word of God says in Psalm 55:22, "Cast your burden on the Lord, and He shall sustain you."

> *1 Peter 5:7*
> *"Casting all your care upon him, for He cares for you."*

We do not have to worry for tomorrow, He is with us!

Do you have fear that God wants to replace with trust? If so, what is your fear?

- Fear that God will not love you?
- Fear that God will not accept you?
- Fear of moving out to express yourself in worship?
- Fear of taking a risk?
- Fear that if you give in the offering you will not have enough for tomorrow?

- Fear of leaving a job, a church or certain relationships?
- Fear of the dark?
- Fear of answering the call God has for you?
- Fear of failure?
- Fear of success?
- Fear of confrontation?
- Fear of standing up for what is right with friends, family or coworkers?
- Fear of _____?
- Fear that God will not forgive you?

I have good news! God is not mad at you! Fear is a trust issue. Either God's word is true and He is who He says He is, or He is not. Who do you say that He is?

God loves you and desires for us to know His presence at all times and to let His perfect love cast out all fear so we can know Him intimately.

He only wants us to reverence and have a holy fear of Him as our King.

The ultimate example of fear and perfect love working together can be seen in Jesus. He instructed us to fear only God, never to fear man.

We are not to be scared of God, but to have such a reverence for Him that impacts the way we live our lives. Father, we stand in awe of you! This is the quality of a Chayil woman! She shall be praised!

Your Chayil Confirmation:
Unite my heart to fear your name. I am your Chayil woman.

ଔ

~ Chapter Eighteen ~

THE MANY VIRTUES OF CHRIST

There are many virtues in this amazing Chayil woman because there are many virtues in Christ. She has the virtue of Christ's ABILITY.

Ability is the skill or potential to do something. But if ability is not used, it only remains potential. Ability is having what it needs to get the job done.

The Bible says God choose able men and made them rulers. He chose the Chayil men (and women) and made them to be the head over the people... rulers of thousands, rulers of hundreds, rulers of fifties, and rulers of tens.

God chose the able men and made them to be the captain, the head person. He placed them at the top and gave them authority, rulership and dominion.

It is the able Chayil people who get promotions! Are you wanting a promotion at your job or a promotion from your job to your own business? Just let your Chayil abilities and potential be on display.

To be able means you will be able to always endure, overcome and prevail.

Numbers 13:3
"Let us go up at once, and possess it; for we are well able to overcome it."

1 Chronicles 9:13 says they were very able men who were chosen for the work of the service (ministry) of the house of God. What has God called you to do in His house?

Don't worry about who you think may have overlooked you! God sees that you are able and He will place you in the body to serve as He sees fit.

Exodus 18:21 says the able men were people who feared God, they were trustworthy people who lived by the truth of God and they hated covetousness, meaning they hated dishonest gain.

These are the virtues of the Chayil woman. We are Chayil women of ability. God has given us potential and we are well able to rise to the top and be displayed for the Glory of the Lord!

She is a woman who possesses the virtue of ACTIVITY. Activity is something that is done for a particular purpose.

Genesis 47:6b
"And if you know any men (women) of activity (Chayil) among them, then make them rulers over my cattle.

She is a virtuous SOLDIER. Soldiers are those who enlist in the army to be a warrior.

2 Timothy 2:3
"Therefore. endure hardness, as a good soldier of Jesus Christ."

She is part of a virtuous Chayil COMPANY. A company is an army of servant worshippers assembled to fight.

Psalm 68:11
"The Lord gave the word: great was the company of those that published it."

This is translated as many women or a great host of women who spread the good news. This is not speaking of a group of wimpy women, but strong Chayil women filled with the Spirit and power of Almighty God.

We are called to be a company of women who go out before the Lord, proclaiming the Word of power that the Lord has spoken.

The virtue of a Chayil woman is GREAT.

To be great means to make large in body, mind, estate or honor. To advance, boast, exceed, excellent, increase, lift up, magnify, nourish or promote.

1 Chronicles 29:12
"Both riches and honour come of thee, and thou reignest over all; and in thine hand is power and might; and in thine hand it is to make great, and to give strength unto all."

The virtuous Chayil woman has GOODS. She is bountiful, joyful, kind, and lives a life of prosperity.

Deuteronomy 28:11
"And the LORD shall make thee plenteous in goods, in the fruit of thy body, and in the fruit of thy cattle, and in the fruit of thy ground, in the land which the LORD sware unto thy fathers to give thee."

She is a part of the Lord's virtuous HOST. A host is an army of worshippers organized for war. He is the Lord of hosts.

Psalm 148:2
"Praise ye him, all his angels: praise ye him, all his hosts."

She is full of the virtue of MIGHT. This means she has the wisdom and power to be a champion.

1 Chronicles 12:8
"And of the Gadites there separated themselves unto David into the hold to the wilderness men of might, and men of war fit for the battle, that could handle shield and buckler, whose faces were like the faces of lions, and were as swift as the roes upon the mountains;"

She has the virtue of RICHES. Riches means to have wealth.

Proverbs 22: 4
By humility and the fear of the LORD are riches, and honour, and life.

She is virtuous and STRONG. She will courageously seize, conquer and prevail.

Joshua 1:7
"Only be thou strong and very courageous, that thou mayest observe to do according to all the law, which Moses my servant commanded thee: turn not from it to the right hand or to the left, that thou mayest prosper whithersoever thou goest."

SUBSTANCE is part of her virtue in Christ. Substance means property and goods.

Proverbs 8:21
"That I may cause those that love me to inherit substance;
and I will fill their treasures."

Chayil also means to have the virtue to TRAIN. Train means to discipline.

Proverbs 22:6
"Train up a child in the way he should go: and when he
is old, he will not depart from it."

We are WORTHY only because of this virtue of Christ in us! Worthy means to be a great, mighty, champion and steward, suitable or deserving of praise.

1 Kings 1:52
"And Solomon said, If he will shew himself a worthy
man, there shall not an hair of him fall to the earth: but
if wickedness shall be found in him, he shall die."

Each of these are qualities of the Chayil woman!

Your Chayil Affirmation:
Christ is my virtue. His life is in me.

ൔ

Chapter Nineteen

THE VIRTUE OF CHAYIL ACCELERATION

We are in a season of giving birth. It's been held back for a long time but a season of new life and abundance is upon us. There is a radical remnant of Chayil women who are pregnant with the dreams and visions of the Lord.

- ൔ We are pregnant with the purposes of God in the earth.

- ൔ We are pregnant with an awakening revival for our family, our city and our nation.

- ൔ We are pregnant with a harvest of souls.

- ൔ We are pregnant with signs, wonders and miracles that must be released into the earth.

Some of these dreams and visions have been passed through the generations but have yet to be birthed.

In this day, at this time, God is doing something that will literally deliver nations. Entire people groups will be delivered in this hour as God brings forth what He's put in the hearts of His people.

This is the time for supernatural Chayil acceleration!

This is the season when His power is being released into the earth for a divine, supernatural, Chayil acceleration of force.

    ❧ An acceleration of wealth...

    ❧ An acceleration of power...

    ❧ An acceleration of strength, might and ability.

The Chayil army is rising and accelerating in the earth.

God wants us to step into His supernatural seasons and cycles of blessings.

Divine acceleration is the supernatural ability of God applied to your life, your ministry, your time and your circumstances, to bring His plans to pass at a much faster rate than is humanly possible.

That is what I call supernatural Chayil acceleration! When our God is at work, nothing can stop Him.

When you step into this place of Chayil force, you will step into an unstoppable momentum that shifts your circumstances, removes obstacles and commands progress in your life.

What is supernatural acceleration and how do we step into it? First - everything about God is supernatural and since He put Himself in us, we are supernatural. Since we are supernatural, why do we act natural?

From now on, let's not vacillate between natural and supernatural. No more struggle between our divine nature and our humanity. Amen? Do you agree? Let's stop trying to bring God down to our level.

Sometimes our actions, words...contradict what we say we

believe. Let's begin to think like supernatural Chayil women, made in the image of Almighty God, whose price is far above rubies.

Let's train our brain - reset our thought processes. Remember. Chayil force is way of life. It is how we live!

God's original intent was for Him to rule in heaven and for us to rule in the earth.

We read in Psalm 110 that this is the day of His (Chayil) power and the Lord shall send the rod of His strength out of Zion so we can rule in the midst of our enemies.

The rod of His strength means the ruling power. His ruling power is connected to His strength.

Strength is the Hebrew word oz...which means praise, boldness, loud, might, power, strength, force. So His ruling power is connected to praise!

> *Proverbs 31:17*
> *"She girdeth her loins with strength..."*

It is the same word, oz, meaning boldness, loud, might, power, strength, force. This strength is like a belt around us. Verse 25 says, "Strength and honor are her clothing." It is the same word, oz, meaning praise boldness, loud, might, power, strength, force.

She girds her loins with praise! Praise is her garment. It is what the Chayil woman wears. She never parts from it.

So what happens when Chayil women praise? Supernatural acceleration takes place!

The human brain is programmed to understand and rationalize things. But that is not how the supernatural realm operates.

Praise creates an open portal between heaven and earth, between God and man.

Why? because praise and worship are both eternal and not confined by time. That means that at its essence, praise and worship are supernatural and was always meant to have contact with the supernatural.

> *Acts 16:25*
> *"And at midnight Paul and Silas prayed, (worshipped) and sang praises (celebrated God): and the prisoners heard them."*

And suddenly. (the earth reacted) so that the foundations of the prison were shaken: and immediately all the doors were opened, and every one's bands were loosed."

Paul and Silas were not quiet, they were not still. I believe that they were giving it everything they had, praising God with their whole heart, body, soul, spirit.

In the natural, they would have had to wait for a trial. But they didn't have time for that! So they praised God and supernatural acceleration took place. Praise opened a portal that created such an unstoppable momentum that even the earth reacted!

Praise is so supernatural, that it may not make a lot of sense to our carnal minds but God can supernaturally open any prison door and let the captives go free!

David was a Chayil man who understood this principle. I believe that is why he said:

Psalm 34:1, 3
"I will bless the Lord at all times. His praise shall continually be in my mouth.

O magnify the LORD with me, and let us exalt his name together."

When you open your mouth and accelerate your praise, the heavens open, revelation and manifestation comes, deliverance comes.

Verse 4
"I sought the LORD, and he heard me, and delivered me from all my fears."

Creation groans for the sons of God to release new levels of praise into the earth realm. It's time to step into supernatural Chayil acceleration.

What is it that you are believing to see manifest in your life?

Begin to praise and thank God for it. Let the strength of praise be your clothing! Wear praise!

Gird your loins with praise and watch for the accelerated manifestation of what you are believing God for!

That is why the rest of verse 25, Proverbs 31 says, "She shall rejoice at the days to come." She will not worry about the future! She laughs without fear at the future!

I believe that is why she was able to accomplish so much!

ᗏ I know she was praising God while she was caring for her husband.

    ೞ I know she was praising God while she was rising at night to care for her household.

    ೞ I know she was praising God while she was buying the field.

    ೞ I know she was praising God while she was planting her vineyard.

    ೞ I know she was praising God while she was giving to the needy.

I started by saying we are in a season of giving birth. Giving birth to praise is what is going to cause the acceleration to take place for the manifestation of the purposes of God in the earth.

Amos 9:11:12
"God will raise up the tabernacle of David and cause us to possess..."

The Tabernacle of the Chayil man David is where praise and worship was first set in order. The word possess means to occupy by driving out previous tenants, and possessing in their place. It means to seize, to rob and to inherit. It also means to expel, to ruin, to cast out, to consume, to destroy, to disinherit and to dispossess without fail.

Lucifer was the anointed cherub created to cover the throne of God with worship. When he fell, the very thing he was created and purposed to do, God now gives that privilege to us and uses it as a weapon against him!

Praise will shut the mouth of the destroyer. Clothe yourself with it. Step in to a place of no more delay through your praise!

Many of you are meant to open businesses - praise your business open! Many of you are called to write books! Praise God in advance and see that book manifest! Many of you are called to step into new dimensions in ministry. Begin to praise God and watch God move on your behalf!

As you begin to praise God, He will show Himself strong in your situation.

Begin to praise God for His promises over your family, your ministry and over your life! Put God in remembrance of His Word though your praises!

God has given us a powerful key called praise. We have been given keys of authority and revelation. When praise, authority and revelation become a three-fold cord, supernatural acceleration takes place.

These keys are being released at an accelerate rate to unlock plans and purposes in regions and territories.

The key of praise has the divine ability to bring the release of blessings in the spirit that have seemingly been locked away. These blessings have not been locked away from the children of God but reserved for the children of God.

Although there has been a "timing element" upon some of these plans, those who have been mantled with the assignment to unlock are being released with the keys and will step into a His divine timing and alignment.

Things that would take three years will take three months. Things that would take three months can be accomplished in three days. And things that would take place in three days can be accomplished in three hours.

In this season, God is writing great exploits upon the hearts of His people. He is releasing dreams and pictures of destiny to strengthen your faith and unlock your potential.

This is the time of supernatural acceleration! This is not the season to be stuck in the memories of past disappointments.

Someone is saying, "Well, I praised God before. It didn't work." God is saying His timing is perfect. Praise Him again!

It is time to stop seeing through the lens of limitation. The exploits of God are about to accelerate upon the earth and unlock His plans for us. It is time for supernatural, Chayil acceleration! Your praise will release it so praise, praise, praise!

Your Chayil Affirmation:
I am a Chayil woman and I praise my way
into divine acceleration.

ଙ

~ Chapter Twenty ~

THE VIRTUE OF THE CHAYIL MANDATE

As women, we carry a lot. We carry children, family, husbands and jobs. As we grow older, we carry our parents. We care for the household, we work, we serve. Yes, we keep the world running. I had the wonderful privilege to care for my parents before they transitioned to heaven. It wasn't always easy, but it was always a joy!

The Chayil woman of Proverbs 31 is a perfect example. She does a lot on a daily basis!

But God has made sure that we have everything that we need to live an abundant life and fulfill His good plans for us, even in the midst of all that we face from day to day.

God reassures us that we can do everything we were created and purposed to do!

> *2 Peter 1:3*
> *"According as his divine power hath given unto me all things that pertain unto life and godliness, through the knowledge of him that hath called me to glory and virtue:"*

Jeremiah 29:11
"For I know the thoughts that I think toward you, says the LORD, thoughts of peace, and not of evil, to give you an expected end."

God has plans for us. It is our assignment to find out what His plans are and to fulfill them!

We each have a Chayil mandate from God. All of us are a force! We all have virtue. We all have abilities! Strength! Power! Might!

Whatever sphere we have been sent into, we must fulfill our Chayil mandate through Jehovah Chayil!

A mandate is an official order or commission to do something. We are not just little church members, born to warm a pew. Each of us has been given an official order from the King to change atmospheres and rule our world! We each have a specific Chayil mandate that nobody else can fill. It will take faith for you to fulfill your mandate.

We have been given a key called faith. Faith is a key to unlock the next dimension of your mandate. We all have faith but God wants us to have strong faith.

Romans 4:3
"Abraham believed God, and it was counted unto him for righteousness."

Verses 18-19
"Who against hope believed in hope, that he might become the father of many nations, according to that which was spoken, So shall thy seed be.

And being not weak in faith, Abraham staggered not at the

promises of God through unbelief; but was strong in faith, giving glory to God;

>*Verses 21*
>*"And being fully persuaded that, what he had promised, he was able also to perform."*

You can be weak in faith or you can be strong in faith. Strong faith doesn't care what the situation looks like! Strong faith believes God.

>*Genesis 18:14*
>*"Is anything too hard for God?"*

>*Mark 11:22*
>*"And Jesus answering saith unto them, Have faith in God."*

Not faith in people. Not faith in money. Not faith in your family. Not faith in your pastor.

Have Faith in God because He who has called us is faithful!

Faith has eyes to see, therefore, faith converts the invisible to the visible. What do you see? If you can see it, you can have it.

As I study more about this woman, I came to realize how much faith it takes to care of family, to be an entreprenuer and to care for others.

That's our Chayil mandate! We will accomplish it only one way - by faith! We need faith to please God.

Faith is the key!

Hebrews 11:6
"But without faith it is impossible to please him: for he that cometh to God must believe that he is, and that he is a rewarder of them that diligently seek him."

Faith is how we live!

Hebrews 10:38
"Now the just shall live by faith."

We need faith to fight.

1 Timothy 6:12
"Fight the good fight of faith..."

This means that the only way we can win in life is with faith. We need faith to overcome.

1 John 5:4
"And this is the victory that overcomes the world, even our faith."

Ephesians 6:16 tells that above all, we must take the "shield of faith" to quench all the firefly darts enemy throws at us. So we need faith to stop enemy!

I looked up the word shield. It is not talking about a small shield. The reference is on a large door shaped gate. What is the biggest door you can see? That is the size of your shield. So to accomplish our mandate, it will take faith.

Jesus said, "...According to your faith be it unto you."

Matthew 9:29
"Then touched he their eyes, saying, According to your faith be it unto you."

What is your "it?"

Since the Kingdom functions by faith, and faith is the order of the Kingdom, let's allow our faith to increase in order to meet the level of God's ability!

Nothing is impossible with God!

Faith says that which God has promised, He is able to perform. See Numbers 23:19.

Let's go from faith to faith, not worry to worry. Worry is negative faith. Negative faith produces anxiety, fear, doubt and worry.

- Negative faith is still faith.

- Negative faith is faith in a negative outcome.

- Negative faith thinks and expects the worst instead of thinking and expecting what God has said.

You must refuse to have negative faith - no matter what it looks like! We are strong CHAYIL women with a mandate -

If God says, your mandate is to be a Chayil force and change the healthcare system, or open a business or start a ministry, will you move in faith or will you say to yourself, " I can't do that?"

- Negative faith will tell you that the healthcare system has been in place a long time. It will be impossible to change it.

- Negative faith will tell you that you cannot open a business because nobody knows you.

- Negative faith will tell you that you cannot start a business because you don't have the connections or the resources.

If you listen to negative faith, you will talk yourself out of your mandate instead of living in the force, ability, strength, might, wealth and power of Chayil faith!

We must learn to live in a gated community. In expensive neighborhoods, certain houses are behind a gate and can only be accessed through the gate. In fact, you have to have a code to get beyond the gate.

As a Chayil woman, make sure your mind is well guarded. Put your mind in a "gated" place so that the code required to access your thoughts is faith. Let faith be your code and let faith guard your mind so you can fulfill your mandate.

You are the only thinker in your head. You are the only voice speaking to your mind. I heard someone say, "Check yourself, don't wreck yourself."

There are enough people who doubt you. Do not add your name to the list. Take your name off of your list of doubters.

Let your thoughts be a place of faith. They will manifest into action.

$\mathfrak{R}\mathfrak{O}$

CONCLUSION

The second part of Proverbs 31:25 says, "...She shall rejoice in time to come." Another translation says, "She shall laugh without fear at the future."

That is the confidence God wants every Chayil woman to have in Him. He is our virtue. He is our praise. He is our force. He is our strength. He is our wealth. He is our ability. He is our everything!

Everything came from Him and it is in Him that we "...live, and move and have our being." Acts 17:28

Let's look at a few more Chayil scriptures.

Judges 6:12, God appears to Gideon and called him a "mighty man of (Chayil) valor."

In Genesis 47:6, Pharaoh says to Joseph:
> *"The land of Egypt is before thee; in the best of the land make thy father and brethren to dwell; in the land of Goshen let them dwell: and if thou know any men of (Chayil) activity among them, then make them rulers over my cattle."*

Exodus 18:21-22
"Moreover thou shalt provide out of all the people (Chayil) able men, such as fear God, men of truth, hating covetousness; and place such over them, to be rulers of thousands, and rulers of hundreds, rulers of fifties, and rulers of tens:

And let them judge the people at all seasons..."

The rulers were considered as the head person of any rank or class, a captain that had rule, a chief, a general, a governor, a keeper, a lord, a prince or a steward. They had dominion.

Deuteronomy 3:18
"And I commanded you at that time, saying, The LORD your God hath given you this land to possess it: ye shall pass over armed before your brethren the children of Israel, all that are meet for the (Chayil) war.

Psalm 84:7
"They go from (Chayil) strength, to (Chayil) strength, every one of them in Zion appears before God."

Habakkuk 3:19
"The LORD God is my (Chayil) strength, and he will make my feet like hinds' feet, and he will make me to walk upon mine high places."

Daniel 4:34-35
"And at the end of the days I Nebuchadnezzar lifted up mine eyes unto heaven, and mine understanding returned unto me, and I blessed the most High, and I praised and honors him that liveth for ever, whose dominion is an everlasting dominion, and his kingdom is from generation to generation:

And all the inhabitants of the earth are reputed as nothing: and he does according to his will in the (Chayil) army of heaven, and among the inhabitants of the earth: and none can stay his hand, or say unto him, What doest thou?"

1 Samuel 16:18
"Then answered one of the servants, and said, Behold, I have seen a son of Jesse the Bethlehemite, that is cunning in playing, and a mighty (Chayil) valiant man and a man of (Chayil) war, and prudent in matters, and a comely person, and the LORD is with him."

He calls each of us to cross over and enter into the promises He has for us as Chayil women! This is not a movement, it's a lifestyle. Let's be bold and strong! Let's live in the power of His virtue in us! Chayil!

Your Chayil Affirmation:
I will fulfill my God ordained mandate
because the virtues of Christ are in me!

℘

International Company of Chayil Women

Please join the International Company of Chayil Women (ICCCW). We are forcefully advancing to carry God's glory to the nations.

- The purpose of the ICCW Chayil Global Initiative is to empower and activate women all over the world to discover their virtue through the Chayil anointing.

- The International Company of Chayil Women is a network of women committed to empowering ourselves so we can empower others.

Through our Facebook page, we will provide coaching, inspiration and encourage local ICCW meetings to connect in order to meet the needs for other women in your city, state or nation.

Look us up on Facebook and let us know if you would like to join or be an ICCW Chayil Agent in your city, state or nation.

We are destined to change the world - one woman at a time!

#empoweringourselvesempoweringothers

ABOUT ICCW

Our first foundational scripture is Proverbs 31:10:
"Who can find a virtuous woman? for her price is far above rubies."

Our second foundational scripture is Psalm 68:11:
"The Lord gave the word: great was the company of those that published it.

Psalm 68:11 could read as follows:
The Sovereign Master appointed, ascribed, assigned, charged, delivered, directed, distributed the promise. Abundance and mighty is the army of worshiping, servant soldiers organized for war that cheerfully announced, preached and published good tidings.

Our third foundational scripture is Psalm 110:1-3:
"A Psalm of David. The LORD said unto my Lord, Sit thou at my right hand, until I make thine enemies thy footstool.

The LORD shall send the rod of thy strength out of Zion: rule thou in the midst of thine enemies.

Thy people shall be willing in the day of thy power, in the beauties of holiness from the womb of the morning: thou hast the dew of thy youth.

Power is the word CHAYIL - This is the day of His Chayil power and we are His willing ones, ready to take dominion, advance His kingdom and rule in the midst of our enemies.

How to join ICCW

We believe that aligning with ICCW involves building a relationship. Our goal is to equip and empower women who can equip and empower others. Here are the steps you can take if you choose to start an ICCW chapter in your area.

1. Pray about connecting with ICCW for the purpose of making a difference in the lives of the women God puts in your sphere of influence.

2. Email us at intlccw@aol.com so we can know that you are interested in starting a ICCW Chapter in your city, state or nation. We will train you and commission you.

3. Be sure to join us for ICCW Facebook broadcasts. If you cannot join us as we go live, be sure to go back and watch the broadcast at your convenience.

4. Feel free to let us know how we can stand with you in prayer. Forward any prayer requests to intlccw@aol.com.

5. Please read and study the Chayil booklet that will be emailed to you to become familiar with the scriptural meaning of Chayil. Study Proverbs 31 so you can know who we are as Chayil women. Be sure to teach the basic principles of Chayil as found here in the pamphlet and on the Facebook broadcasts. This way, we will be sure to lay the foundation together.

6. You can request an ICCW team to come minister in your city, church or region. We frequently lead teams or send teams to minister in various locations.

7. As a leader, you will gather women in your sphere. Please pray about the day, time and place to host a Chayil Power breakfast, Chayil Power lunch or Chayil Power dinner. You may also want to host a Chayil Power Outing for fellowship or for outreach.

    You may feel free to meet in your home or at a local restaurant. Many restaurants have meetings rooms that can be used at no charge. You will only need to call to reserve the room. When you meet, be sure to empower the women with the foundations of the truths of Chayil which can be found throughout the word of God.

NOTE: Please adhere to the teachings of Chayil only.

Also, please see the Leader's Report Form and submit it prior to and following your ICCW meeting.

Once you choose your date, time and place, please let us know. Together we can gather the army and change nations! Always be sure to ask ladies to join the Facebook page.

We also recommend that you spread the word as a Chayil kingdom witness by getting some of our Chayil products. They make great conversation starters! Request the Chayil Order form to place your order.

Spread the word. We are on a mission for a global take over - empowering ourselves to empower others!

Let's be the army of the Lord who joins forces to establish and advance His kingdom!

ॐ

- About -

Dr. Pamela Scott

PAMELA SCOTT is an ordained minister, a preacher / teacher of the Word of God. She received a Master of Fine Arts degree in dance and a Doctor of Ministry degree from FICU in Merced, California. Pamela has danced on Broadway in New York City and performed in national and regional touring productions.

Ordained as an Apostle, Dr. Pamela travels throughout the U.S. and abroad. God has sent her to over 23 countries. She is a frequent guest minister at churches, seminars and conferences. Apostle Pamela is called to minister a Rhema word to worship teams, ministry networks, as well as in the area of women's concerns. She is the founder of the International Company of Chayil Women and the Junia Company for five-fold women ministers.

Apostle Pamela is the founder of Eagles International Training Institute, (www.eaglesiti.org), an accredited, on-line international training school, serving and soaring for 17 years in over 20 countries. EITI provides a School of the Arts, a School of Business and a School of Theology, with over 20 online courses to train and equip the body of Christ. She also serves as Founder of Eagles Nest Global, a network for ministry leaders.

Pamela is the founder of TEN (The Eagles Network – Worldwide) www.tenworldwide.org. TEN also has a presence in over 20 countries.

Dr. Pamela is the author of:
- ✆ "I Am Chayil"
- ✆ "Unlocking Your Prophetic Destiny"
- ✆ "Dance: The Higher Call"
(Available in English and Spanish)
- ✆ "Act Now! A 31 Day Devotional To Activate, Cultivate And Transform Your World"
- ✆ "Let The Nations Rejoice
An Invitation To Dance"
- ✆ Journeys of Eagles Who Soar
An anthology project with graduates of EITI

As a former pageant winner, Dr. Scott has started Image1Enterprises, home of the "Inspired Pageant and Celebration" for young girls 7-17 throughout the Dallas Ft. Worth Metroplex. IPAC inspires them to see their potential and to celebrate their dreams.

She is aligned with Dr. Chuck Pierce at Glory of Zion Ministries, located at the Global Spheres Center in Corinth, Texas.

She is the Founder and Director of Set Free Evangelistic Ministries.

CONTACT DR. SCOTT:

214-402-9647 / DrPamela3126@gmail.com
www.eaglesiti.org / www.tenworldwide.org

www.ingramcontent.com/pod-product-compliance
Lightning Source LLC
Chambersburg PA
CBHW051718090426
42738CB00010B/1970